Art & Technique of
Scandinavian-Style
WOODCARVING

by Harley Refsal

Fox
Chapel Publishing

1970 Broad Street • East Petersburg, PA 17520
www.FoxChapelPublishing.com

Art & Technique of Scandinavian-Style Woodcarving,
published in 2004 by Fox Chapel Publishing Company,
Inc., is a completely revised and updated version of the
author's original text titled *Woodcarving in the
Scandinavian Style* (Sterling, 1992). This new edition
features digitally scanned photographs and line
illustrations; new step-by-step photographs of carving and
painting Oskar, which replace the previously published
step-by-step photographs; the addition of a second step-
by-step demonstration on carving and painting a horse in
the traditional Scandinavian folk art style; and the
addition of 20 new patterns.

Publisher	Alan Giagnocavo
Book Editor	Ayleen Stellhorn
Editorial Assistant	Gretchen Bacon
Cover Design	Jon Deck
Step-by-Step Photos	Greg Heisey
Layout	Blue Mammoth Design

ISBN 1-56523-230-5

Library of Congress Control Number: 2004106143

To order your copy of this book,
please send check or money order
for the cover price plus $3.50 shipping to:
Fox Chapel Publishing
Book Orders
1970 Broad St.
East Petersburg, PA 17520

Or visit us on the Web at
www.FoxChapelPublishing.com

Printed in China
10 9 8 7 6 5 4 3 2 1

Acknowledgments

The Swedish Institute (Stockholm), Döderhultarn Museum (Oskarshamn), Norwegian Foreign Ministry (Oslo and New York), Norwegian Folk Museum (Oslo), Viking Ship Museum (Oslo), Nordmanns-Forbundet (Oslo), Norway-America Association (Oslo), Maihaugen (Lillehammer), Akademiet (Rauland), E.L.C.A.-Faculty Research Grant (Chicago), Sons of Norway (Minneapolis), American-Swedish Institute (Minneapolis), Vesterheim (Decorah) and Luther College (Decorah) have all provided me with financial and/or moral support in connection with my research. To them as well as to my family, friends and countless other museum staffers, librarians and woodcarvers, I extend my sincere appreciation.

Except in the step-by-step demonstrations and as noted otherwise, all of the photographs were taken by Chip Peterson (or me), and all of my carvings were painted by my wife, Norma Refsal.

Table of Contents

About the Author

Harley Refsal is a professor of Scandinavian Folk Art and Scandinavian Studies at Luther College in Decorah, Iowa. He is an internationally recognized figure carver, specializing in Scandinavian-style flat-plane carving.

Refsal was born and raised on the farm near Hoffman, Minnesota, homesteaded by his Norwegian-immigrant grandparents. He began working in wood as a young boy. His father, a carpenter and farmer, and a woodworker uncle who lived nearby kept him well supplied with wood, tools and encouragement.

Primarily self-taught, Refsal began winning awards in regional and national carving exhibitions by the late 1970s. He also began researching the history of Scandinavian flat-plane carving, with which he had become especially enamored. But soon he discovered that most of the artists who had worked in this style during the height of its popularity in the early decades of the 20th century in both Scandinavia and America had died and the tradition of flat-plane carving had faded to near-extinction.

Since the 1980s, Refsal, who speaks fluent Norwegian, has shared his knowledge of, and skills in, Scandinavian flat-plane carving with

Harley Refsal sometimes dons a traditional Scandinavian-style work shirt when he carves.

thousands of carvers in classes and presentations in the United States and Scandinavia. In addition to writing several books on the subject, he has authored many book chapters and magazine articles. His name is so integrally linked with the revival of this carving style that it is often referred to as the "Refsal style."

In 1996 he was decorated by the King of Norway, receiving the St. Olav's Medal for his contributions to Norwegian folk art.

Preface

In this book, the discussion of Scandinavian-style figure carving, and "flat-plane" carving in particular, will deal with a style of carving that developed and became popular in Norway and Sweden. Although Denmark, Finland and Iceland also comprise part of Scandinavia, I am limiting the discussion to Norway and Sweden since their conditions and traditions are fairly similar — especially, as we shall see, when it comes to figure carving. Therefore, in the context of this book, the term "Scandinavian" will refer only to Norway and Sweden. The style of figure carving I will be discussing was common in both countries, but it was far less common in Denmark and Finland and nearly non-existent in Iceland.

The term "flat-plane carving" stems from a particular style of figure carving — one in which large, flat planes, created by using primarily a knife and perhaps just a gouge or two, were left intact. Smooth, rounded sculpting and sanding were typically not employed in the final finish.

I was introduced to Scandinavian figure carving during my first visit to Norway in 1965. Two years later, while studying at the University of Oslo, I was able to travel more widely throughout Norway as well as in Sweden. Since I had worked with wood and had also done some whittling as a boy, I became interested in the woodcarving traditions of both countries. I was especially intrigued by the small wooden figures I saw in shops and museums.

Upon returning to the United States in 1968, I began to carve figures of my own, using a pocketknife and a wood chisel that my father, a carpenter and farmer, had made from a worn-out file. Since I was unable to locate any carvers creating the style of figures I had seen in Scandinavia, I simply gleaned what information and inspiration I could from photos, articles and sketches I had made.

One of the articles I eventually ran across featured photos of some carvings by Axel Petersson Döderhultarn, whose rough-hewn figures have made a lasting impression on me. Using only a few well-placed cuts and leaving large flat planes, he was able to convey fascinating stories in wood.

I had been attempting to tell stories through my figures too, and Döderhultarn's style of carving provided just the means of expression I had been seeking. I began using this style of carving to create objects and figures with which I was familiar, and I began trying to say more by saying less.

Since that first visit in 1965, I have traveled in Norway and Sweden on many occasions. By the early 1980s, however, I noticed that fewer figures carved in this flat-plane style were available in shops.

Meanwhile, I had been carving a great deal in the United States and teaching courses and workshops on Scandinavian-style figure carving since the early 1980s. So when my family and I moved to Norway in 1988, where I was enrolled in a graduate program of folk art studies, I was

eager to explore the figure carving tradition further. I also hoped to locate carvers who were still creating figures in this style. But I eventually learned that the tradition had become almost extinct, and I couldn't locate a single course being taught on the subject, either in Norway or Sweden.

Therefore, when I was asked if I would teach a weeklong course at the school I was attending, I readily accepted. Since 1988, I have taught numerous courses and workshops in Norway on flat-plane carving and am pleased to see that there is now a growing number of Scandinavian, as well as American and Canadian, carvers who are carving once again in that style.

During the year my family and I lived in Norway, I traveled throughout Norway and Sweden, gathering additional information about the tradition and its practitioners. I am happy to be able to share with you in this book what I have learned.

After having taught courses throughout the United States as well as in Scandinavia, I can't decide which I enjoy more, carving figures myself or trying to help others develop their skills so that they can tell their own stories in wood. But I can say with certainty that my admiration for the small wooden figures that whispered into my ear over twenty-five years ago only keeps on growing.

—Harley Refsal

CHAPTER ONE

The History of Scandinavian Figure Carving

❖

Before focusing our attention on Scandinavian figure carving, it is important to consider the general context in which this particular folk art emerged. As we shall see, wood chips were flying in Scandinavia long before figure carving became popular there.

VIKING ERA AND MEDIEVAL CARVING

Our earliest examples of woodcarving in Scandinavia date back to the Viking era (ca. 800-1050 A.D.). Already back then, woodcarving had reached a high level of achievement, as indicated by the items found buried with the Oseberg Ship, now housed at the Viking Ship Museum in Oslo. The Oseberg Ship was named after the Norwegian farm that was on the land from which the ship was excavated. Buried with the ship were vehicles and furniture and all kinds of household and personal items. Thus, the excavation, conducted in 1904, yielded a unique look into the past, providing us with a time capsule thought to date from the first half of the ninth century.

The items decorated with carving include the ship itself, a horse-drawn carriage and three sledges. In terms of the motifs, there are relief-carved animal ornamentations, geometric designs and some three-dimensional figure carving. The high quality of the carving from the Oseberg excavation suggests that woodcarving must have been a leading form of art in the Viking era.

Another excavated Viking ship, the Gokstad Ship, can also be seen at the Viking Ship Museum. Dating from around 900 A.D., this ship also contained some carved items, including parts of a bed frame that features the relief-carved head of an animal, possibly a horse. In addition, the head of an animal or beast of some kind, carved three-dimensionally, appears on one of the ship's oar-locks. Both the bed frame and the oarlock were rendered in a mode of carving that has become known as the Borre style. Named after a burial mound on a Norwegian farm called Borre, this style was widespread both in Norway and Sweden.

Wooden stave churches (named for the large staves, or pillars, in their support structure), built in Norway from ca. 1000 to 1300 A.D., also featured examples of woodcarving. Of the estimated one to two thousand stave churches once found throughout the country, only about thirty have survived. But decorative carving from these churches provides us with yet another excellent source of Norway's rich carving heritage. Animal and plant motifs, especially around doorways

Horse and Rider, 1830. (Lårdal Bygdemuseum, Telemark).

Relief-carved head on a bed frame, from the Gokstad Ship (Viking Ship Museum, Oslo).

Animal head post from the Oseberg find (Viking Ship Museum, Oslo).

Oseberg Ship (Viking Ship Museum, Oslo).

and on pillars, were common. The motifs often blended native and foreign elements, drawing some of their impulses from classical traditions common throughout other parts of Europe.

The carving found on stave churches as well as from earlier Viking era ship finds was undoubtedly done by trained artists, some of whom may have worked under royal patronage. As the stave church era progressed, local carvers may have also been trained on site to do some of the carving, but most of the work from this period was done by specialists, not by "common folk" who simply picked up a tool and began to carve.

The tools available to Viking era carvers certainly must have included gouges and curved knives in addition to simple straight-carving, or all-purpose, knives. It is impossible for the intricate relief work found in the Oseberg excavation as well as on stave church portals and doors to have been done using only a knife. A woodcarving tool from the Middle Ages found in an excavation near Tønsberg, Norway, suggests that a wide variety of tools had been developed and were available to carvers at that time. Therefore, we must conclude that similar tools were available several hundreds of years earlier as well.

There is very little evidence of "art for art's sake" from the Viking era. Some small figures, carved primarily in bone, ivory or stone, which were undoubtedly of cultic or religious significance, have been discovered. Also, a few gaming pieces, such as the carved-ivory chess pieces known as the Lewis Chess Set (now in the British Museum in London), have been found. But, in the main, the carving during the Viking era was decorative or applied art on functional objects.

It is, of course, possible that carved wooden objects, including figures, were far more common than the evidence suggests. But due to the nature of the material, wood, most would have rotted away long ago. However, one excavation site at Kvivik on the Faroe Islands, settled by Scandinavians during the Viking era, has yielded two tantalizing wooden horses and two small wooden boats, probably created for use as children's toys. One can only speculate about the identity of the carver, or carvers, of these objects. The simplified, almost crude, pieces could certainly have been carved with only a knife, so perhaps just a "common person," handy with a knife, created them.

On the whole, however, the rich carving tradition, practiced in Scandinavia approximately seven hundred to a thousand years ago, was carried on by trained artists. Yet, as we shall see, their work lived on to inspire countless self-taught craftsmen, who studied the Viking era and medieval motifs and began replicating them on their farms and in their homes.

FROM STAVE CHURCH TO STOREHOUSE: THE EMERGENCE OF FOLK ART

Scandinavia, along with much of the rest of the world, was ravished by the Black Death, or bubonic plague, in the mid-fourteenth century. It is estimated that over half of the population died, after which large parts of Scandinavia, especially Norway, were laid waste for several generations. Artistic development was severely curtailed, as the people were devastated and had to spend virtually all their time simply eking out a living. It wasn't until a couple of centuries had passed that the people were back on their feet to the extent that they could think about devoting time to aesthetically enhancing their surroundings.

The populations of Norway and Sweden have historically been overwhelmingly agrarian. Only a very small percentage of the people lived in towns, a situation that remained true well into the nineteenth century, when the Industrial Revolution began to create jobs in factories. Prior to that, most people lived on self-sufficient farms, where all their buildings, vehicles, tools, furniture and utensils were made of wood, right there on the farms.

At least well into the eighteenth century, Scandinavian farmers were largely illiterate, had no formal art training, lacked travel opportunities and had few, if any, pictures or books at their disposal. So, farmers who wanted to decorate a building or household object turned for inspiration to designs they saw firsthand in their own communities. In some parts of Sweden, inspiration could have been drawn from nearby manor

Detail from doorframe, Gol Stave Church, ca. 1200 (Norwegian Folk Museum, Oslo).

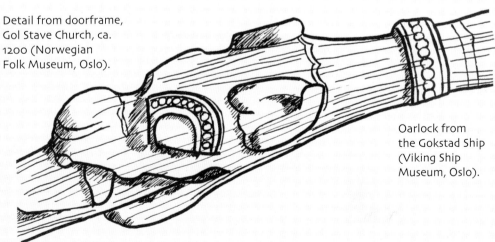

Oarlock from the Gokstad Ship (Viking Ship Museum, Oslo).

houses or castles. In other parts of Sweden, as well as in Norway, inspiration often came from churches. After viewing a professionally carved candle holder, baptismal font, pulpit or portal, countless farmers returned to their homes and modeled drinking vessels, candle holders, utensils or other household objects on what they had seen. In Sweden, and especially in Norway, with its numerous ornately carved stave churches, farmers began to replicate pillars and doorways from churches on their storage buildings, virtually all of which were made of logs. Carved ornamentation also began to appear on their houses.

In addition to scroll-like plant motifs and geometric designs, majestic and daunting images of animals figured prominently in architectural carving. Lions were especially common. Originally a symbol of kingship in the Orient, the lion motif made its way, with returning crusaders, to the European continent where it became a common element in heraldry. Over time, the theme was picked up by other artists on the Continent, including carvers, and eventually lions found their way into Scandinavian design—first as deep-relief carvings mounted on doorposts of stave churches and later on storage buildings, furniture and tools.

This phenomenon of untrained artists adopting the designs and motifs of earlier artists and then reinterpreting and creating them in their local setting is a good example of what we now call "folk art." Folk art was also referred to as "peasant art" early in the 20th century, since it was typically made by rural folk of meager means who had to create and decorate their possessions themselves, rather than purchase them. In the Scandinavian context, folk art was basically the art used on utilitarian objects, including everything from buildings and vehicles to utensils and toys, that was created by the people in the

Eidsborg Stave Church, Telemark, Norway, ca. 1300.

general population, who drew their inspiration from the designs they saw around them.

Two main types of art existed simultaneously during this "Golden Age of Scandinavian Folk Art" (ca. 1700-1850). Urban or "international" art thrived among the rather small upper class, while more of a peasant art flourished in the heavily populated rural areas.

It is of interest to note that from the sixteenth through the eighteenth century, farmers and other rural craftsmen who were creating folk art had relatively few tools at their disposal. Specialized tools for carving, fine woodworking and joinery were jealously hoarded by the small groups of urban craftsmen, most of whom were in the guild system. In Norway, a royal decree from the

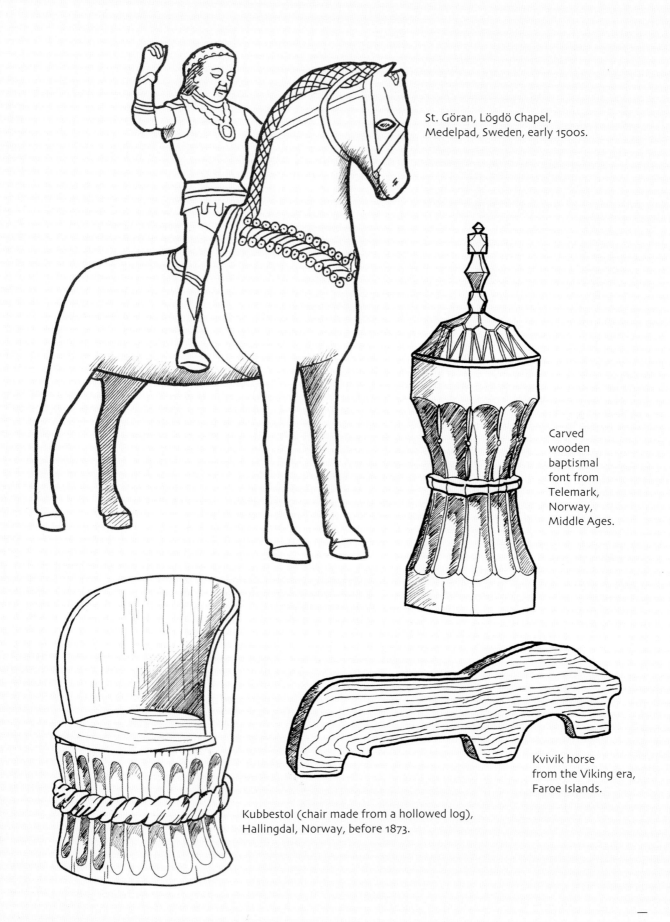

St. Göran, Lögdö Chapel,
Medelpad, Sweden, early 1500s.

Carved
wooden
baptismal
font from
Telemark,
Norway,
Middle Ages.

Kvivik horse
from the Viking era,
Faroe Islands.

Kubbestol (chair made from a hollowed log),
Hallingdal, Norway, before 1873.

Craftsman with knife and axe.

Carving tool from the Middle Ages, found near Tønsberg, Norway.

Viking era carver (drawing by Uwe Rudolf).

Pieces
from the
Lewis Chess Set,
made of walrus
ivory, 1200s
(British Museum,
London).

Danish king (Norway was under Denmark's rule from 1380 to 1814) actually made it illegal for farmers throughout the country to use refined tools. In an effort to thwart competition with the trained craftsmen of the government-controlled guild system, farmers were forbidden to use tools other than knives and axes—tools deemed sufficient for basic but rough construction of log buildings, simple furniture and farm implements. Many farmers obviously ignored the decree, which was in effect for about a hundred years, from the late seventeenth to the late eighteenth century, and made or bartered for fine woodworking tools. Still the ban was somewhat effective, and much of the work done by rural craftsmen during that era reflects the limited range of tools at their disposal.

However, if one has only a couple of tools available, one can develop amazing skill with just those tools, and some highly impressive work was created during that period with just a knife and an axe. The story is told in the Norwegian county of Telemark about a man who was seeking employment as a log builder. Having just wandered into a community, he was directed to a site where a log building was under construction. The man approached the foreman about a job, but the foreman was hesitant and asked the stranger if he could handle an axe. Without saying a word, the stranger walked over to a chopping block, spread apart the fingers of his left hand and laid it palm-down on the block. He then proceeded to chop into the block four times, striking the axe perfectly in the spaces between his outstretched fingers. When he was finished, the foreman said, "You can start right over there on the far corner!"

Log storehouse, Telemark, Norway.

Lion detail on portal of Eidsborg Stave Church, Telemark, Norway, ca. 1300.

Contemporary rendition of traditional Norwegian knife and sheath, made by Norma Refsal, 1989.

WOOD: THE UNIVERSAL MATERIAL

Norway and Sweden are richly endowed with forests. Nearly half of Sweden and a quarter of Norway are covered with pine, spruce and birch. Due to the cool climate afforded by the Scandinavian Peninsula's northerly latitude, trees grow slowly and are typically not harvested until they are seventy-five to one hundred and fifty years old. Annual growth rings are therefore close together, providing ideal material for woodwork of all kinds.

Almost everything was made out of wood in traditional, rural Scandinavian society. In addition to buildings and vehicles, objects that we today regard more as hardware items, such as hinges, pails, tools and fending materials, and even shoes were made primarily from wood.

Instead of searching for a tree that would provide that "nice, straight board," farmers and craftsmen often chose a suitably curved or twisted piece instead. A branch from a gnarled mountain birch tree that had been deformed through years of buffeting by wind and snow might yield just the perfect shape from which a hinge, C-clamp or plow beam could be made. A naturally bent limb with the grain following the shape is, of course, stronger than a piece of wood that one could create into that shape artificially. Thus, a plow beam made from a six- to seven-inch-thick, naturally bent birch branch fitted with an iron tip proved to be nearly as strong as one made entirely from metal.

Burls were also widely used. The grain in a burl does not run in only one direction but appears to swirl around almost randomly, so burls provided ideal material from which to carve bowls and scoops.

Bowls were often turned on a lathe, but freeform shapes were also created, carved from a crotch or a burl. Ale bowls, sometimes carved in

Wooden plow with iron plowshare (Rauland, Telemark, Norway).

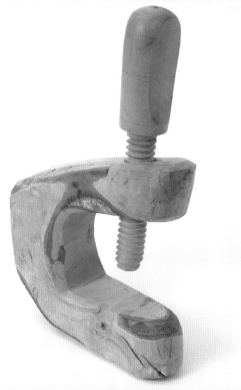

Bent birch tree
(Rauland, Norway).

C-clamp, made from a naturally formed piece of birch
(Rauland, Norway).

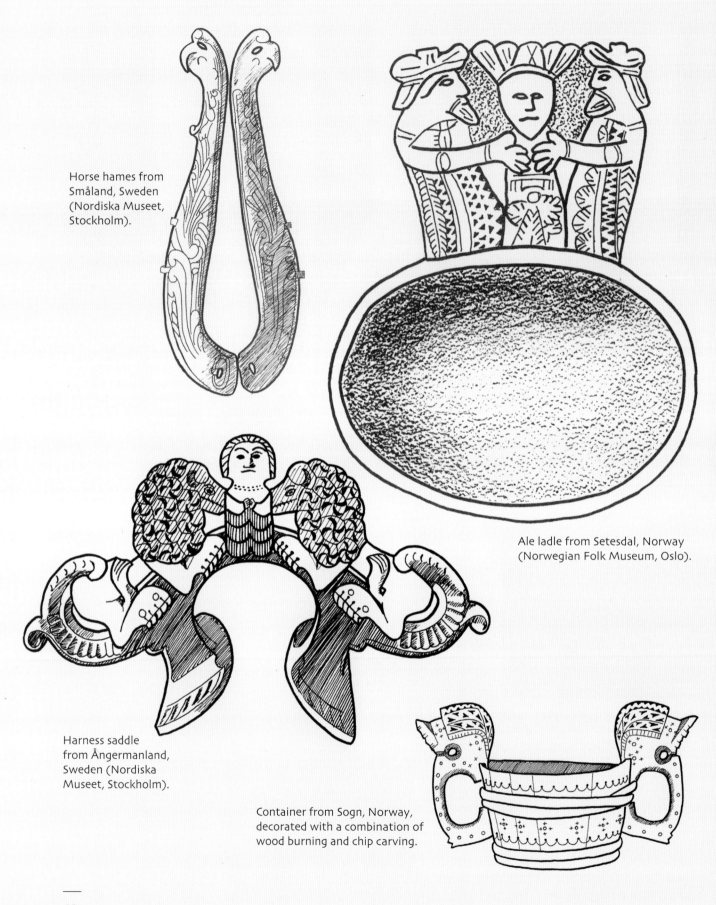

Horse hames from
Småland, Sweden
(Nordiska Museet,
Stockholm).

Ale ladle from Setesdal, Norway
(Norwegian Folk Museum, Oslo).

Harness saddle
from Ångermanland,
Sweden (Nordiska
Museet, Stockholm).

Container from Sogn, Norway,
decorated with a combination of
wood burning and chip carving.

the shapes of hens or geese, were used for ceremonial drinking, especially in connection with weddings, funerals and other ceremonies or festivities. Some bird-shaped ale bowls were carved with rounded bottoms, and they would be floated on the surface of the ale in a larger wooden container. They served as floating dippers, from which one could either drink directly or pour the ale into another container.

Due to their ceremonial use, ale bowls were frequently decorated with carving or painting. Other bowls, however, were often shaped according to the piece of wood from which they were carved, with the shape itself providing the design.

Horse hames or other harness fittings and parts were also made using naturally bent or curved pieces of wood—preferably birch, because of its strength—and were frequently decorated as well. The harness saddle shown on page 12, originally from a farm in the Swedish province of Ängermanland and now on view at the Nordiska Museet, Stockholm, is a good example of the use of a naturally curved piece of wood. A component of the harness also exemplifies the use of the lion motif that was mentioned earlier.

Clogs, or wooden shoes, provide yet another example of articles commonly made from wood.

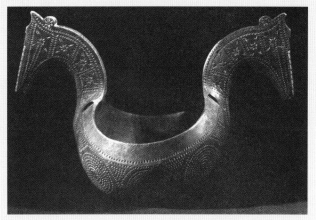

Norwegian ale bowl, possibly late eighteenth century (Vesterheim/Luther College Collection, Decorah, Iowa) (photo: Darrell Henning).

Although we associate wooden shoes primarily with Holland, clogs have been worn since the Middle Ages in many parts of Europe, including Norway and Sweden. Even after the introduction of the more expensive leather boots and shoes, wooden clogs continued to be popular since they could be made locally and were so convenient. You simply stepped into them and walked off. Clogs were often lined with hay or straw, both for cushioning and for warmth. The pair pictured here, believed to have been made in Scandinavia and brought to the United States by immigrants who settled near Hoffman, Minnesota, was even fitted for winter traction, complete with hand-forged metal spikes on the bottom.

Many of these articles, intended for everyday use, were decorated. Employing chip carving, relief work, incised carving and/or wood burning, traditional craftsmen transformed hinges, drinking vessels, ladles and harness parts into articles that were also aesthetically pleasing. "The eye also has its needs" is an expression that craftsmen regularly took to heart.

As we can see, even though it is difficult to document a figure carving tradition per se within Scandinavian folk art that goes back more than a few hundred years, the stage had been set long

Wooden shoes, with metal spikes on the bottom.

before. Wood had been a universal material for centuries. It would only be a matter of time before craftsmen familiar with the material and skilled with knives would begin turning their attention to carving objects other than just utilitarian items.

THE EMERGENCE OF CARVED FIGURES

The earliest carved human or animal figures in this folk art tradition were probably used as protective or good-luck charms. Some were mounted inside houses, whereas others stood guard in storage buildings.

Two figures from a farm called Heggtveit Vestre in Telemark, Norway, are noteworthy examples of such charms. One of the figures, a *husgud* (house god), approximately six inches tall and featuring the head of a human, was originally fastened high up on the interior wall of the house. Believed to date from the Middle Ages, it is one of the oldest and finest examples we have of a house god in Norway. It resembles the kind of figure, perhaps a saint, commonly found on walls or pillars inside churches.

The second figure, a horse and rider, pictured on page 3, was prominently placed as a protective or good-luck charm on the second floor of the Heggtveit farm's storehouse. The 1830 date painted on the horse's stomach, together with the rider's dress, suggests that the figure represented a government official or military man, perhaps attached to the Telemark Company in nearby Dalen. In 1830, Swedish military uniforms were being worn in Norway, since Norway was united with Sweden from 1814 to 1905. The rider's outstretched hand has a small hole drilled through it, indicating that some object, perhaps a flag on a flagpole, was originally part of the carving.

A candle holder in the form of a lion (see page 17) now in the Sandvig Collection at Maihaugen in

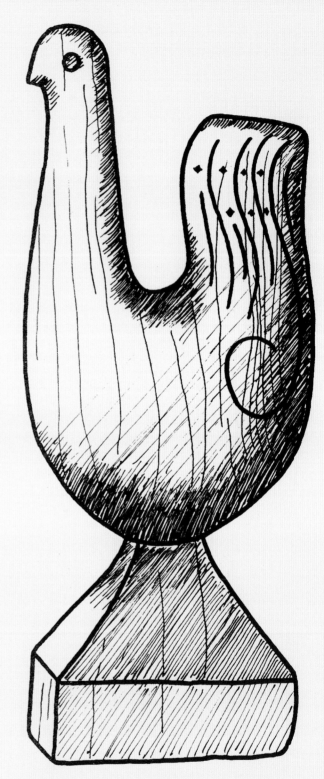

Rooster from Dalarna, 1840s (Nordiska Museet, Stockholm).

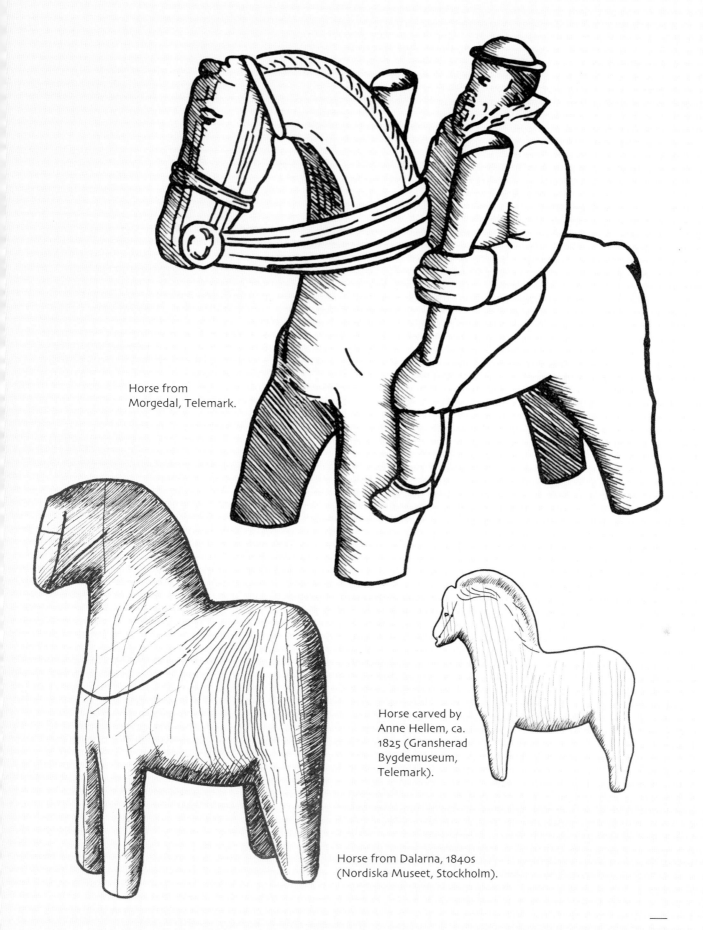

Horse from
Morgedal, Telemark.

Horse carved by
Anne Hellem, ca.
1825 (Gransherad
Bygdemuseum,
Telemark).

Horse from Dalarna, 1840s
(Nordiska Museet, Stockholm).

Lillehammer, Norway, harks back to the lion motif that was mentioned earlier. The piece was originally from a farm near Ringebu in Gudbrandsdalen.

Another figure in the Maihaugen Collection, an elegant horse, made by the famous eighteenth-century carver Kristen Erlandsen Listad (1726-1802), is technically a toy but one of those toys that children undoubtedly had to handle very carefully. The Listad horse was featured in a commemorative stamp in 1987, the one-hundredth anniversary of the Sandvig Collection.

Another horse (pictured on page 15) was carved in approximately 1825 by Anne Hellem of Gransherad, Telemark. This carving, also undoubtedly created for use as a toy, is fairly unique in that it was made by a woman. Carving, as well as woodwork in general, was typically done by men, whereas women devoted themselves more to textiles.

The carving of wooden animals and human figures by common folk in Sweden is traceable back more than two hundred years. It can readily be documented since about 1840, with the emergence of the now-world-famous Dalecarlian horse, an object that has become Sweden's unofficial national symbol. The province of Dalarna, and especially the community of Mora, had long been a center for the building of wooden clock cases, and the horses whittled from the scraps leftover from the clock cases gradually became an economic mainstay for countless families.

Even earlier than the 1840s, however, men working in lumber camps often lived far back in the woods and were separated from their families for weeks or months at a time. As a way of using their free time during the long winter evenings and in order to be able to bring home toys for their children, the men often whittled horses or

Doorframe detail on storehouse, Telemark, ca. 1300 (Norwegian Folk Museum, Oslo).

other figures. Although roosters and pigs were not uncommon objects, horses were favored by carvers as well as by the children who received them. These figures, some of which can be seen in the Nordiska Museet in Stockholm and in various provincial museums, were painted in colorful floral motifs or sometimes left unpainted. The horse from Dalarna shown on page 15 was originally painted, but years of use by small hands have nearly obliterated the coloration and given it a warm, dark patina.

As previously mentioned, it was near Mora that large-scale production of the Dalarna figures began in about 1840. The carving of the figures, primarily horses, was done by local craftsmen in their homes. Working in pine or spruce, a good carver could produce a dozen horses per day, using a hatchet and a knife as his only tools. Flat-plane carving, with visible tool marks, was the result. The figures were usually left unsanded.

Candle holders from Östergötland, Sweden
(Nordiska Museet, Stockholm).

Candle holder from Ringebu,
Gudbrandsdalen, Norway,
now at Maihaugen, Lillehammer.

Horse carved by Anne Hellem, ca. 1825.

The painting was done by specialists who often drew their inspiration for designs from the horses featured in the well-known wall paintings in the area. Many of these wall paintings seem to have received their inspiration from illustrations in the so-called "Gustav Adolf's Bible" of the 1580s. The styles of saddles and martingales, as well as the combination of colors chosen by the painters of the wooden horses, suggest that wall paintings significantly influenced many of the painters.

It is interesting to note that as long ago as the 1840s the Dalecarlian horse had already become a popular item throughout Sweden. When Mora area craftsmen traveled by horse and wagon to other parts of the country to sell their locally produced clocks, baskets or spinning wheels, they typically had along a good supply of carved horses, which they used as payment for their room and board. The figures thus became a kind of currency. Frequently the horses, which were meant to be used as toys, were given to the children of the farmer or innkeeper with whom they stayed. In addition to paying for lodging, the horses were also commonly traded for such items as seed or wool. Upon returning to Mora, the craftsmen, in turn, sold the goods for cash.

Frequently other salesmen would come to Mora and buy up large quantities of carved horses to use as gifts, barter items or payment for room and board as they traveled throughout the country selling their wares. Although it is not known exactly how much they had to pay for the horses, it was, at any rate, cheaper for them to pay for their lodgings with wooden horses than to use cash, and apparently the horses were readily accepted as payment wherever they traveled.

Demand for the horses became so great, therefore, that large-scale production became common—even in the 1840s. As noted earlier, the carving was done by craftsmen, and specialists did the painting. Anders Nisser, the son of the well-known, early twentieth-century painter Mor Nisser, estimated that he had to shoot as many as fifteen to twenty squirrels per year just to keep his mother supplied with enough squirrel hair to make the brushes she used to paint the horses.

The production of Dalecarlian horses has continued right up to the present. Since 1928, nearly all the figures have been made in and around the village of Nusnäs, near Mora. Although modern technology is now used both in sawing out the figures and in some aspects of the

Toy horse from Øyfjell Bygdemuseum, Telemark.

The world-famous Dalecarlian Horse.

painting process, each figure is still carved by hand by local craftsmen and receives its painted decoration by hand as well. Not only are the horses sold in Sweden and throughout the rest of Europe, but they are also sent to shops in Japan, Australia, Canada and the United States.

It is clear that there has been a folk art tradition of carving small human and animal figures for at least the past two to three hundred years, especially in Sweden. Three-dimensional figures were sometimes created as part of a decorative whole (lions on doorposts, for example). Other figures were carved as freestanding utilitarian objects (toys, human figures used as candle holders, bird-shaped drinking vessels and so on). Still other figures were created as pieces of representational, nonfunctional art, but they were probably made by carvers who found figure carving to be nothing more than an enjoyable pastime. And then along came Axel Petersson Döderhultarn. . . .

CHAPTER TWO

Scandinavian Figure Carvers

❖

Among a long list of Scandinavian figure carvers, several stand out. It is these outstanding carvers to whom we now turn our attention.

AXEL PETERSSON DÖDERHULTARN

Axel Petersson has been called a natural genius. He was born in the parish of Döderhult near Oskarshamn in 1868. His figures, which typically depict the peasants and village folk around whom he grew up and lived, have earned him the reputation of one of Sweden's greatest artists.

Even as a boy, Petersson exhibited considerable artistic talent both at home and in school. His talent was never encouraged, however, and his only training stemmed from a brief informal apprenticeship under a local woodcarver and sculptor, Edward Källström. His primary interest lay in whittling or sculpting small figurines, an activity considered a worthless pastime by his neighbors as well as his family.

His family finally decided that young Axel should emigrate to America, where he would be forced to stand on his own two feet and make something of himself. So money was provided, and off he went. But he didn't get farther than nearby Malmö, where instead of purchasing a ticket to America, he spent most of his travel money on lottery tickets and partying.

Upon his return to Oskarshamn, where his widowed mother had moved in 1889, he continued his figure carving. Much to the dismay of his family and acquaintances, carving remained his primary activity. For nearly twenty years, he lived in relative isolation, venturing out only occasionally to attend social gatherings or to sell his inexpensive wooden figures at the local market in Oskarshamn.

As he had been taught by Källström, Petersson carved in a rather naturalistic style during the beginning of this period. His early work, often in pear wood and rendered in quite a traditional style, was typically sanded. Although the style of his work defies a systematic chronology, sometime around 1900 he developed more of a rough-hewn, flat-plane or minimalist style. Using a knife and just a few gouges, he began carving figures in alder. Upon completion, many of his figures were then painted in subdued colors.

Petersson's six- to fifteen-inch-tall figures portray local peasants engaged in everyday activities: milking a cow, attending a funeral, wedding or baptism, having their picture taken by a photographer and so forth. It's been said that he also derived inspiration from medieval wooden sculptures in churches, caricatures drawn by the famous Swedish artist Albert Engstrom and illustrations in various publications, including some that were Norwegian.

Saturday Night by Bjarne Walle.

Axel Petersson Döderhultarn

Left: Axel Petersson Döderhultarn (Döderhultarmuseet, Oskarshamn) (photo: Ataljé Lindblad). Top right: Boys playing with carved wooden figures, including two of Döderhaltarn's. Photo from the archives of Döderhultarmuseet, Oskarshamn, ca. 1913. Above: Army Horse, by Döderhultarn (The American-Swedish Institute, Minneapolis, Minnesota).

Döderhultarn in his studio (Döderhultarmuseet, Oskarshamn) (photo: Ataljé Lindblad).

In 1909 Petersson was invited to participate in a caricature exhibition in Stockholm. Public response to his work was immediate and overwhelming. In the newspaper *Dagens Nyheter* (News of the Day) on January 20, 1909, art critic Georg Nordensvan wrote: "Axel Petersson's old men are irresistibly amusing. They depict such primitive art as one could wish for, made out of a couple of simple contours using only a couple of strokes, but, from an artist with sure eye and nimble hands. It is a new conception

Finger Hooking, by Axel Petersson Döderhultarn (The American-Swedish Institute, Minneapolis, Minnesota).

with a personal touch . . . small masterpieces of complete nonconformative art." As can be said of a great cartoonist or caricaturist, he had mastered the difficult art of simplification—saying more by saying less.

Following closely on the heels of the exhibition in Stockholm, some of Petersson's figures were purchased by Swedish art museums, lending even further legitimacy to the artistic merit of his work. He also began receiving requests to have his work exhibited throughout the rest of Europe and

in the United States. Hailed as "Döderhultarn" (the man from Döderhult), he started using that name in addition to Axel Petersson.

In 1910 his work was shown in Paris. In 1911 it was exhibited in Brighton, Copenhagen, Rome, Turin, Stockholm and Malmö. Fifty-seven figures were also shown in Oskarshamn, and a museum association was formed there to lay the groundwork for a Döderhultarn Museum. In 1912 some of his work was shipped to the United States, where the Swedish Consulate sent it on a

Axel Petersson Döderhultarn

Dancers, by Axel Petersson Döderhultarn (Döderhultarmuseet, Oskarshamn) (photo: Sven Nilsson).

tour of several cities, including New York, Buffalo, Toledo, Chicago, Boston and San Francisco.

Döderhultarn's prominence as a "high artist" is well documented and accepted. However, at the same time that his work was being exhibited internationally and purchased by museums, he continued to carve figures for local sales.

The photo of the two boys outdoors with the carved wooden figures (on page 22) is from the archives of the Döderhultarn Museum and is believed to have been taken in 1913. The photo suggests that the boys were using the wooden fig-

ures as toys. The two human wooden figures clearly appear to be the work of Döderhultarn. The photo had been mailed, without an accompanying note, to Döderhultarn, possibly as a way of thanking him, or as proof that the figures that had been ordered had arrived and were indeed being used.

Beginning in 1908, Döderhultarn's figures were sold through the Handcraft Association in nearby Kalmar. The store continued to serve as his local sales outlet, even after the artist had achieved international fame.

A postcard sent to Döderhultarn by the store in 1915 features a photo of the store's interior, showing several of the artist's carvings on the counter. On the back of the postcard, the store placed yet another order with the carver. Individual figures sold for approximately ten *kronor* (U.S. $1.50-$2.00), while groupings sold for thirty to forty *kronor*.

Photos of Döderhultarn's figures were widely circulated. Articles about, and reviews of, his exhibitions often included drawings of his work, and postcards featuring his carvings were available at least as early as 1912, if not earlier.

Peasant, by Axel Petersson Döderhultarn (The American-Swedish Institute, Minneapolis, Minnesota).

Axel Petersson Döderhultarn

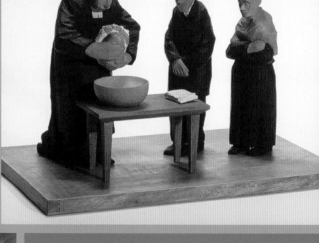

Above: The Christening, by Axel Petersson Döderhultarn (The American-Swedish Institute, Minneapolis, Minnesota). Left: Detail from The Christening. Top: Wedding, by Axel Petersson Döderhultarn (Döderhultarmuseet, Oskarshamn) (photo: Sven Nilsson).

It has been said that Döderhultarn was unique. It seems that his uniqueness lay not in that he was one of the first to carve figures in this style, but rather in that he was the first essentially self-taught figure carver to be accepted or discovered by the art world. Döderhultarn stood firmly planted in the world of folk art, carving wooden figures destined for use as children's toys—but he also carved similar figures for exhibition in art museums and galleries throughout Europe and America.

Döderhultarn's influence on other carvers

Döderhultarn's influence on other carvers should not be underestimated. Since photos and drawings of his work were so readily available and widely circulated, they undoubtedly served as inspiration for countless other carvers in Scandinavia and abroad.

A "Döderhultarn figure" became a generic term for any small wooden figure rendered in a minimalistic style. For example, a souvenir stand near Oskarshamn hung out a sign some years ago advertising Döderhultarn figures. When asked if the figures for sale were actually carved by Axel Petersson, the proprietor replied that, of course, they weren't carved by Axel Petersson, but because of the style and subject matter, they were indeed Döderhultarn figures.

The simplicity of Döderhultarn's figures comprised an art form with which common folk could easily identify. The people, who had grown up in a tradition in which practically every male was at least somewhat skilled with a knife, apparently felt that they too could create "Döderhultarn figures," even though they may not have had any art training. For instance, in a letter to Döderhultarn in 1922, a resident of a home for the elderly in Sundbyberg, Sweden, wrote that he was looking for a hobby to help pass the time.

Since he had done some woodworking years ago, he said, he was interested in working in wood, perhaps in making some small figures. Then he went on to ask for Döderhultarn's assistance and advice.

The popularity of Döderhultarn's figure carving among common folk quickly spread beyond his own country. Evidence of this can be seen from an article in the September 28, 1913, issue of the widely read Norwegian magazine, *For Bygd Og By* (For Country and Town), which described the work of a figure carver named Ragnvald Einbu from Gudbrandsdalen. The writer, apparently without any need for further explanation to the general readership of the magazine, compared the Norwegian artist to "the well-known Axel Petersson, Döderhultarn, from Småland in Sweden."

Another Norwegian, Sverre Johnsen (1844-1939) created, among other pieces, Döderhultarn-style figures. According to the *Lexicon of Norwegian Artists*, Johnsen was called "Norway's Döderhultarn." Johnsen was, however, only one of many who carved small individual figures or groupings depicting such themes as a drinking party, card players or a chorus and was compared to Petersson.

In the United States and Canada, where hundreds of thousands of Norwegians and Swedes had emigrated only a few decades earlier, figure carving had also become popular. The late Dr. Marion Nelson, professor of art history at the University of Minnesota and former director of Vesterheim, the Norwegian-American Museum in Decorah, Iowa, wrote in 1989: "In doing research . . . it became evident that there was a lot of small figure carving among the Norwegians in our area about 50 years ago. The subjects were immigrant[s] and pioneer[s] . . ."

Despite the lack of written documentation indicating that Döderhultarn's carvings directly influenced other carvers, several of his subjects and designs can clearly be recognized in the work of later carvers. One is obviously Oscar Sjögren, an artist who emigrated from Emmaboda, Sweden, in the 1920s and settled near Duluth, Minnesota. Not only did he create figures in a style reminiscent of Döderhultarn's, but he also featured some of the same subjects, such as a wedding scene and a photographer.

Photos and sketches of pieces by H. S. "Andy" Anderson, the well-known American caricature carver, suggest that he too had seen pictures of Döderhultarn's work. Anderson, in turn, went on to influence other American figure carvers, including Harold Enlow. Enlow states that when he began carving, his initial inspiration came from Anderson's book, *How to Carve Characters in Wood.*

Although many carvers drew much of their inspiration from Döderhultarn's work, this should not minimize in any way their own creativity and artistic talent. Everyone derives inspiration from one source or another. As I have mentioned earlier, Döderhultarn's work has served as an inspiration for my own work as well. It is merely interesting to note that his influence has been enormous and far-reaching—right up to the present.

Petersson was once asked how he felt about other carvers emulating his work. Did he mind? Did he regard them as unwelcome competition? No, he said, he wasn't threatened in the least. "There are thousands of snuffbox carvers out there, but there is only one Döderhultarn!"

CARL JOHAN TRYGG

It has been said that it's often only fate that determines which artist becomes the standard-bearer of a new style of art. Axel Petersson became known as the father of Döderhultarn figures,

but perhaps the figures could have been called "Trygg figures" instead.

Born in 1887 in Skagerhult, near Örebro, C. J. Trygg began carving wooden figures as a boy. As one of nine children in a poor family, he had to quit school and leave home at the age of twelve to earn money to supplement the family's income. But he continued to carve rough-hewn figures that depict the types of folk he knew from his background: primarily Swedish farmers, laborers, preachers, policemen and seamen.

Even though C. J. Trygg began carving figures before Döderhultarn's 1909 Stockholm exhibition, the figures of Trygg, who was nineteen years younger than Döderhultarn, were similar in style to Döderhultarn's and extremely well done.

At first Trygg was unable to make a living from just the sales of his carvings and had to carve on a part-time basis while working at other jobs. But eventually, perhaps in part because of an exhibition of his work in Stockholm in 1915, he was able to devote himself full-time to his carving.

Trygg enjoyed telling a story about the initial purchase of his work by an art dealer in Stockholm. The dealer's wife had wanted her husband to purchase a dozen figures, but the dealer only purchased three. The next day, Trygg, who had never met the art dealer in person, dressed up in his finest and went to the shop, where he promptly bought all three of his own figures. The day after that, the dealer contacted Trygg and ordered two dozen figures. Through the years, this dealer continued to be Trygg's best customer in all of Stockholm.

Together with his three sons, Carl Olof, Nils and Lars, who were also figure carvers, Trygg immigrated to Canada in the 1930s. There, C.J. and sons, especially Carl Olof (born in 1910), apparently met with considerable success. While

Hobo, by C.J. Trygg.

Sailor, by Lars Trygg.

Logger, dated 1930, by C.O. Trygg.

their figures had been earning them only a few crowns each in Sweden, they were fetching up to $20 apiece in Canada.

Both C.J. and C.O. Trygg eventually returned to Sweden, however, where they continued their careers. C.J. is said to have carved well over ten thousand figures before his death in 1954. Much of the Tryggs' work can be found in private collections in Canada and the United States as well as in Sweden.

OSCAR SJOGREN

Born Josef Oscar Sjögren and raised near Emmaboda, Sweden, Sjogren (1883-1964) immigrated to Superior, Wisconsin, in 1922. He was employed as a commercial artist in nearby Duluth, Minnesota, but woodcarving was his lifelong passion. Drawing on memories of friends and neighbors back in Sweden as well as folks from the Duluth-Superior area for his models, Sjogren was yet another carver who created figures in a minimalist style.

Although his figures are somewhat more refined than those of Döderhultarn, they clearly show knife and gouge marks and portray some of the same rural characters and situations featured in Döderhultarn's pieces. His work is represented in numerous private and museum collections. The largest collection of Sjogren figures and groupings is owned by the St. Louis County Historical Society in Duluth, Minnesota.

HERMAN ROSELL

Herman Rosell (born in 1893) was another self-taught Swedish carver who created small figures and groupings that depict rural life in the nineteenth century. His abilities as a carver and caricaturist were highly regarded, and in addition to participating in exhibitions both in Sweden and abroad, his work was featured in a film on Swedish television in 1959.

Although his subject matter is similar to Döderhultarn's, his style of carving is more refined. Rosell has stated that he became familiar with Döderhultarn's work only after he had carved for many years and developed his own style.

In addition to pieces in Sweden, a number of Rosell's figures can be seen at the American-Swedish Institute in Minneapolis, Minnesota.

EMIL JANEL

Born Emil Nygård in 1896 near Orsa, Sweden, this gifted artist began to attract attention even as a very young boy when he started whittling small wooden animals. Despite a lack of any formal training, he continued to carve and paint, and at nineteen years of age was awarded first prize at a national sculpture exhibition in Stockholm.

Recognizing his artistic abilities, both Carl Milles, a well-known Swedish sculptor, and Anders Zorn, a painter, invited Emil to study with them. But the young artist's parents would not allow it, stating that he had to help his father with his job as a woodcutter and part-time ranger.

In 1923 Emil traveled to Winnipeg, Canada, where he joined his brother and began working as a lumberman. Eventually he moved to Seattle and then to San Francisco, where he lived for the rest of his life. It was when he moved from Canada to the United States that he adopted the surname "Janel," after the famous turn-of-the-century sports figure, John L. Sullivan. He had been told that his Swedish name, Nygård, was too difficult and confusing for non-Scandinavians to pronounce.

Working primarily in unseasoned alder, Janel carved his fifteen- to twenty-four-inch figures using only a mallet, gouges and a knife, holding the

Oscar Sjogren

The Male Chorus, by Sjogren
(The American-Swedish Institute,
Minneapolis, Minnesota).

Peasantry Wedding,
by Oscar Sjogren
(from the collection
of the St. Louis County
Historical Society,
Duluth, Minnesota)
(photo: St. Louis County
Historical Society).

Far left: Paul Bunyan, by Sjogren. Top right: The Photographer, by Sjogren. At the Fishmarket, by Sjogren (all from the collection of the St. Louis County Historical Society, Duluth, Minnesota) (photos: St. Louis County Historical Society).

Herman Rosell

Immigrant Couple, by Rosell (The American-Swedish Institute, Minneapolis, Minnesota).

Above: Three Women Having Coffee, by Herman Rosell (The American-Swedish Institute, Minneapolis, Minnesota). Left: Fiddler and Woman, by Rosell (The American-Swedish Institute, Minneapolis, Minnesota).

Seated Man, by Emil Janel (The American-Swedish Institute, Minneapolis, Minnesota).

Detail of Seated Man, by Emil Janel.

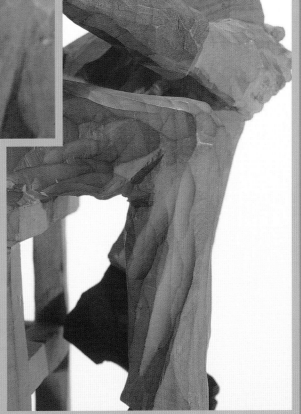

Left: Gunnarsson Seaman.
Right: Man with Cap, by Gunnarsson.

figures between his knees. As with Döderhultarn's and other Scandinavian figure carvers' work, with which he undoubtedly was familiar, Janel's characters, typically tall and thin, depict common folk going about their everyday activities. Frequent subjects were laborers, immigrants and loggers he had encountered. However, he did not carve in an angular, flat-planed, minimalist style, but rather his work has been categorized as "exaggerated realism."

During the first years he lived in the United States, he had to earn part of his livelihood from jobs other than his carving. But eventually he supported himself through his carving alone, especially after he began his association with Maxwell Galleries of San Francisco. In 1965 Janel was awarded the Royal Order of Vasa by His Majesty King Gustav Adolph VI of Sweden in recognition of his work as an artist. He died in San Francisco in 1981.

SVEN AND URBAN GUNNARSSON

When Sweden's late Prime Minister Olof Palme visited Cuba, he brought along a gift for Fidel Castro: a wooden caricature of the bearded Cuban leader, carved by Sven Gunnarsson.

Gunnarsson (1909-1985) began carving figures as a boy. His rough-hewn, flat-plane figures depicted rural folk and clearly recognizable political leaders. "Gunnarsson figures" were also carved by Sven's brothers Nils and Olof, and by a son Peder (1936-1968).

In the 1960s Gunnarsson was joined by his son Urban, who was then fifteen. At their shop on Drottninggatan in Stockholm, Gunnarsson figures used to be painted by Urban's mother, Ursula, and are now painted by his sister, Gisela.

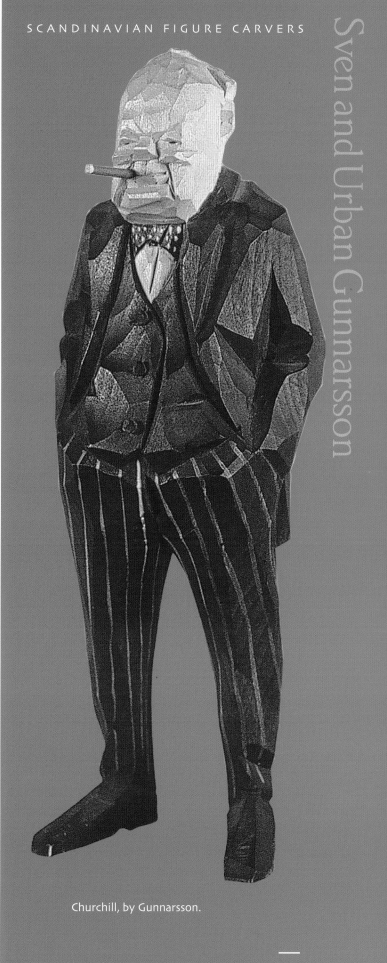

Churchill, by Gunnarsson.

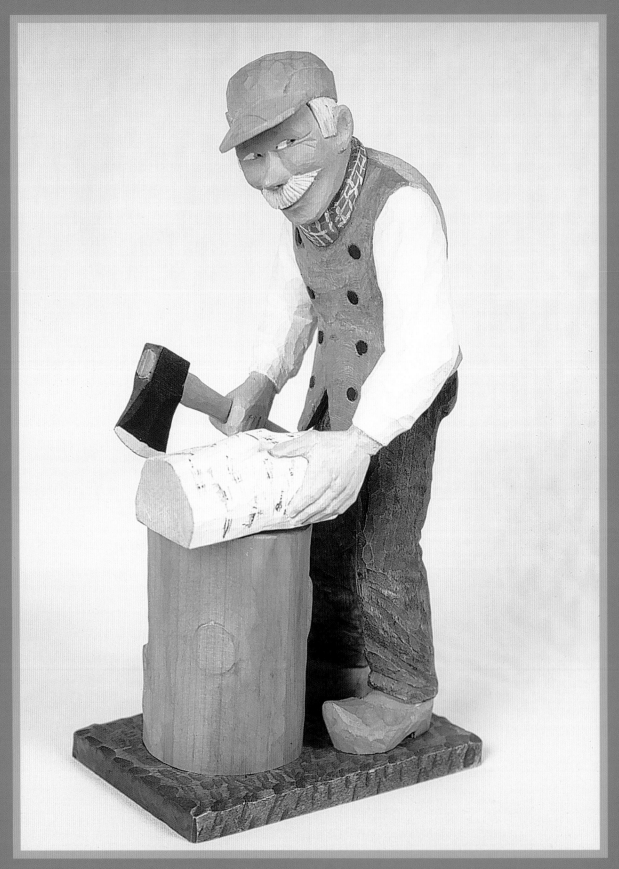

The Woodchopper, by Engseth (photo: Darrell Henning).

The Wood Gatherer, by Engseth (photo: Darrell Henning).

Henning Engelsen

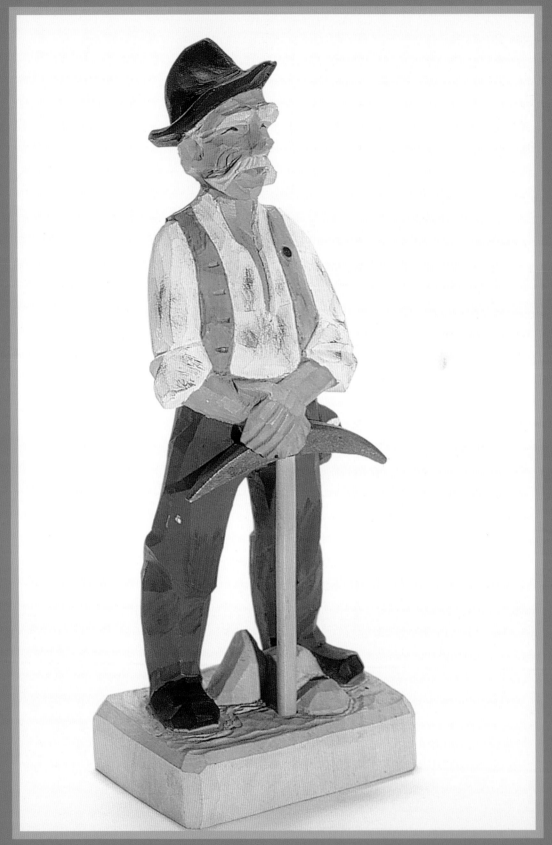

Miner, by Henning.

Henning Engelsen

Top right: Milking Time, by Henning.
Bottom right: Fisherman, by Henning.

MARTIN ENGSETH

Born in Norddal, Møre-Romsdal, Martin Engseth (1903-1972) emigrated from Norway to America in 1926. In addition to working as a *rosemaler* (rose painter), Engseth also carved figures, much in the spirit of other figure carvers of the time in Norway, Sweden and Scandinavian America.

BJARNE WALLE

From the outset of his adult life, Bjarne Walle (1911-1989) wanted to make woodcarving, especially figure carving, his career. Although his flat-plane figures sold for more than 30,000

kroner ($4,000-$5,000) at his first major exhibition in 1945, the artist from Bamble, Norway, also had to work as a carpenter. His desire to tell stories, however, both through his carved figures and his writing, was so strong that he often carved or wrote during his lunch breaks. It was not until 1970 that his income from figure carving and writing allowed him to devote himself full-time to them.

Bottom left: Figure carver Aslak K. Svalastoga, Rauland, Telemark (photo: courtesy of Rauland Dansarring).Top left: Sveinung Svalastoga: porch pillar at Svalastoga home, Rauland, Telemark (photo: Norma Refsal). Top right: Lady with Goat, by Olav Tveito, Vinje, Telemark (Lårdal Bygdemuseum, Telemark). Middle left: Carving by Olav Bakken, Gransherad, Telemark. Middle right: Carving by Kolbein Hommedal, Indre Arna, Norway (from the collection of Nils Kjome, Decorah, Iowa). Middle bottom right: Norwegian Packhorse, by Sjur Mørkve, Voss, Norway (from the collection of Nils Kjome, Decorah, Iowa).

Other Carvers

Right and bottom left: The Tippler, Vesterheim, Decorah, Iowa (carver and date unknown). Top left: Man carved by Anton Pearson, Lindsborg, Kansas (The American-Swedish Institute, Minneapolis, Minnesota). Top center: Woman carved by Anton Pearson, Lindsborg, Kansas (The American-Swedish Institute, Minneapolis, Minnesota).

Walle's painted figures, typically larger and less angular than those of Döderhultarn, often feature trolls or people in humorous situations. His carvings, as with the many stories and books that he wrote, usually have "happy endings." It's been said that Walle couldn't bring himself to allow bad things to permanently befall his characters.

HENNING FIGURES

A carver of trolls, Norwegian rural folk, Vikings, fishermen, animals and characters from Nordic mythology, Henning Engelsen (born in 1918) lives at Kapp, in Toten, about 120 kilometers north of Oslo. He has been creating his flat-plane "Henning figures" since 1947.

His basswood figures, which are popular souvenir items, are sold in shops throughout Norway as well as abroad, especially in the United States. The Henning staff includes about a dozen people, a third of whom rough out the figures by machine. Surface carving is then done by hand by another group, after which the pieces are painted.

Harley Refsal

Top: Half-hour Before Sunup, by Refsal. Right: Firewood, by Refsal.

OTHER CARVERS

The list of carvers whose work has just been reviewed does not even presume to be complete but merely provides a sampler. If we were compiling a complete list, figure carvers such as Gudleik Brekhus, Styrk Fjose, Ragnvald Einbu, Axel J. Persson, Sverre Johnsen, L. Larssen, Hans Sorken, Telle Rudser, "Ole the Hermit," John Altenborg, "Grandma Larkin" and countless others would have been included as well.

By the early 1980s, most of the figure carvers who had been working in Döderhultarn's style back in the 1920s and 1930s—probably the height of its popularity—were no longer alive. Only a few bearers of the flat-plane, Döderhultarn-influenced tradition remained.

HARLEY REFSAL

I have included, here at the end of this chapter, a sampling of my own pieces carved in the flat-plane

Top left: Scandinavian Kick Sled, by Refsal. Middle left: Heading Home, by Refsal, 1988. (Both from the collection of Walter and Marcia Sanders, Jamestown, North Dakota.) Right: The New Schoolmaster, by Refsal, 1988.

style. Many of my carvings are based on my knowledge of Scandinavia, both from a historical standpoint and from personal experience, as I have traveled there often.

Harley Refsal

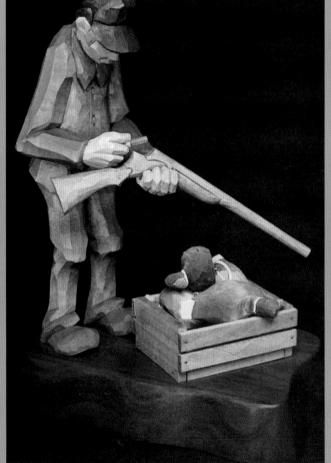

Top left: The Knife Makers, 1989, by Refsal (photo: Arne Aas). Bottom right: Another Season, 1984, by Refsal.

Top left: The Ice Fisherman, 1990 by Refsal. Top right: The Tomte, 1991, by Refsal, painted by Karen Jensen. Bottom right: Nisse Mor and Nisse Far, 1991, by Refsal.

Harley Refsal

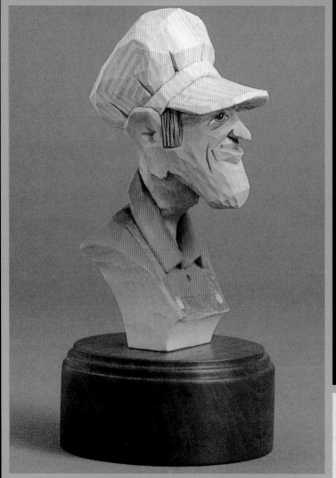

Top left: Farmer, 1987, by Refsal. Top right: The Emigrant, 1989, by Refsal (photo: Arne Aas). Bottom right: Ringer, 1988, by Refsal.

Harley Refsal

Top left: Skiing, 1990, by Refsal. Top right: Woodcarver, 1990, by Refsal. Bottom left: Taming the Prairie, 1987, by Refsal (from the collection of H.M. the late King Olav V of Norway) (photo: Arne Aas).

Harley Refsal

Fjord Horse, by Harley Refsal.

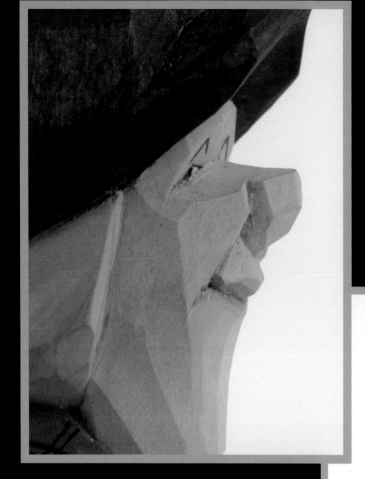

Karl Oskar, 2003, by Refsal. Featured in the video/DVD *Figure Carving Scandinavian Style with Harley Refsal.* (See bibliography page 134.)

Top and left: Father Christmas, 2003, by Refsal. Bottom right: Swedish Rooster (inspired by original, from 1840, in Nordiska Museet, Stockholm), 1988, by Refsal.

CHAPTER THREE

Flat-Plane Carving
Step-by-Step

❖

As you've undoubtedly noticed while reading through the first two chapters, flat plane carvings are just that: carvings that derive their shapes from a series of flat planes.

In this chapter you will be able to follow step-by-step photos, accompanied by explanatory text, as I carve two figures, using only one single knife.

My first project is a stylized horse. Although this critter is my own design, he/she is quite obviously inspired by the traditional wooden horse carved for nearly two centuries in the Swedish province of Dalarna (also known by the Latinized version of that name, Dalecarlia).

It should be noted that the carving of wooden horses was common and popular throughout Scandinavia—not just in Sweden—but it is the Dalecarlian horse that has become the most widely known throughout the world.

Next comes a series of step-by-step photos describing the carving of my old friend Oskar, an immigrant-era figure. If you carefully study the photos and read the accompanying descriptions, you should be able, with just one single knife, to create an Oskar of your own.

Woodcarver, by Harley Refsal.

Carving a Traditional Dalecarlian Horse

1 Choose a block of basswood at least 5½" x 5½" x 1¾". Transfer the pattern (page 128) to the wood and bandsaw the blank according to the pattern.

2 Using a pencil, extend the lines of the front and back legs.

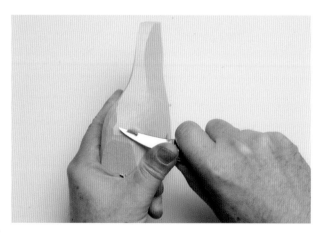

3 Begin removing wood from the back of the horse. Simply round off corners to start.

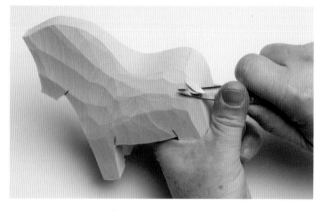

4 Continue removing wood on the sides of the horse to produce a rounded effect.

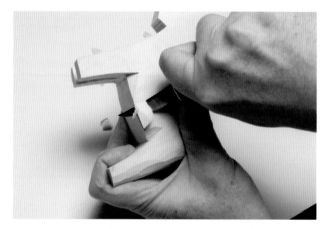

5 Remove wood from the underside of the horse. Remove wood in long cuts to round off the edges.

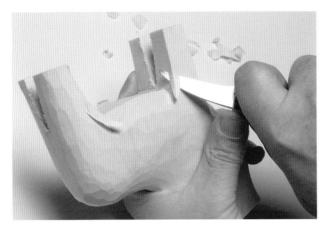

6 Round the legs by removing the corners. Remember, make a minimum of long cuts.

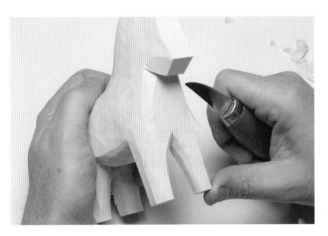

7 When the legs are rounded, move to rounding off the chest.

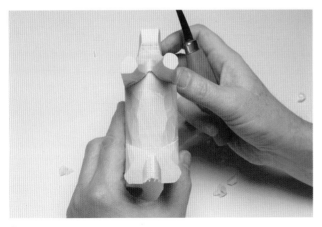

8 A view from the bottom shows how the figure has been rounded. Note that no wood has been removed from the center of the underbelly.

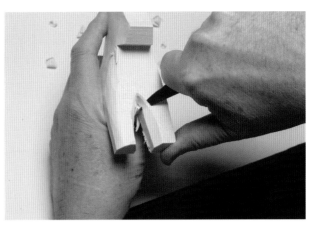

9 Clean up the joint between the front legs and the joint between the back legs.

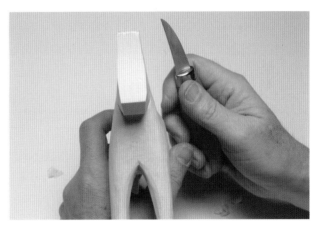

10 A view from the front shows the result of the cuts.

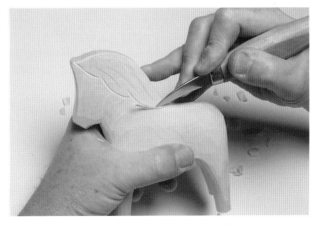

11 Use the tip of the knife to cut in details for the mane and tail.

Painting a Traditional Dalecarlian Horse

1 To paint the body of the horse, start with a 1:5 mix of Ultra Marine Blue Liquitex acrylic paint and water. This is a bright, but thin mix. Test the mix by painting over a piece of newsprint. You should be able to read the words easily through the paint.

2 Begin painting in an inconspicuous area to ensure that the mix is correct. I choose the underside of the horse.

4 The blue paint is dry. Acrylic paint dries very fast, so you'll want to paint the entire surface up to this point in one sitting. Stopping in the middle then restarting may leave an unsightly line where the dry paint meets the wet paint.

3 When you are satisfied with the color, begin to paint the horse. I start at the face and work my way back to the tail. I paint the legs and belly last. The mane and the eye remain unpainted.

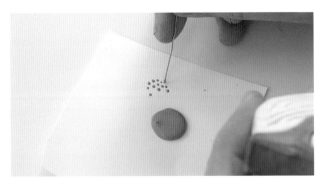

5 I have decided to decorate this horse with polka dots in a contrasting color. The dots are created by dipping the end of a straightened paper clip into a circle of undiluted Pure Orange Plaid Folk Art acrylic paint, then by touching the paper clip to the surface of the horse.

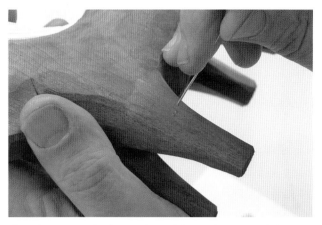

6 When you feel comfortable with your ability to create evenly weighted dots, start to paint the dots on the horse. Begin by making a row of two or three dots about 1/8" apart.

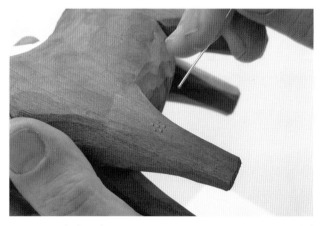

7 Expand the dot pattern to a rosette. Be careful to make the dots as evenly spaced and as evenly shaped as possible. Of course, they won't be perfect, but they should be close.

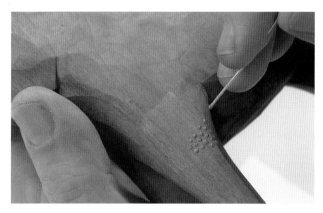

8 Continue adding dots to the surface in a systematic manner.

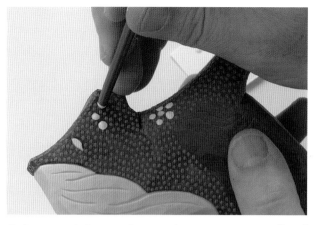

9 Larger dots can be used to create a stylized floral pattern over the dots. Start by dipping the end of a paintbrush into undiluted white paint and touching it to the surface of the horse.

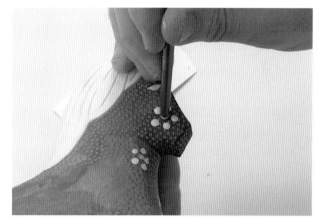

10 Use undiluted yellow paint in the same manner to create the center of the flower.

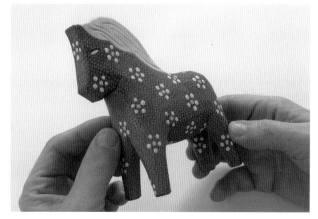

11 Brush on a thin coat of Delta Ceramcoat clear all-purpose sealer. The sealer is optional, but it will help the wood of the unpainted mane and eye to keep its natural color.

The finished Dalecarlian horse.

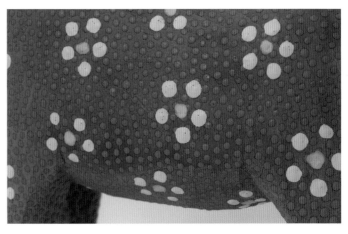

Carving a Traditional Flat-Plane Figure

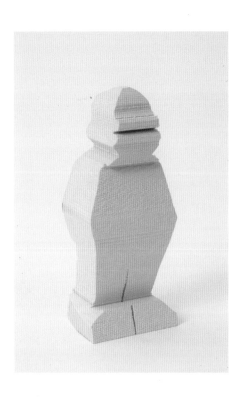

1 Choose a block of basswood at least 6½" x 6½" x 2". Transfer the pattern (page 86) to the wood and bandsaw the blank according to the pattern.

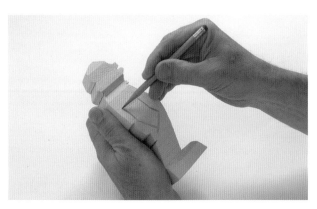

2 On the right side of the blank, draw lines to indicate the position of the right arm. Use the pattern and photographs of the finished piece as guides.

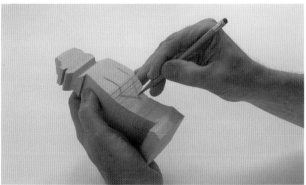

3 On the left side of the blank, draw lines to indicate the position of the left arm.

4 On the bottom of the blank, draw lines to indicate the position of the feet.

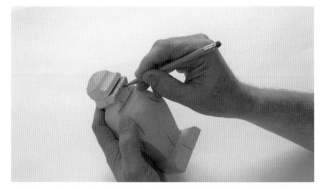

5 On the front of the blank, draw lines to indicate the positions of the facial features, the arms and the legs.

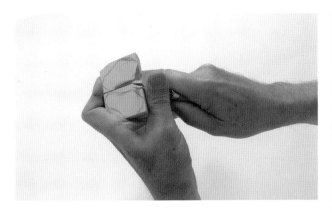

6 Using your thumb for leverage, push the knife blade into the wood, making large cuts to remove the wood around the soles of the feet.

7 Cut in at an angle along the inside of the foot; then cut in from between the legs to meet this cut. The resulting cut will form a triangular-shaped area at the ankles as seen on the left side of the figure.

8 Here you can see how the feet are shaping up. Notice the large, blocky cuts. I am making no attempt to round the feet.

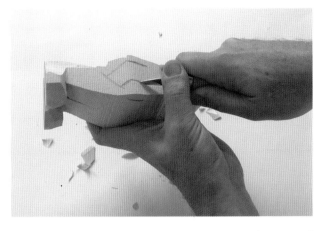

9 Using the tip of the knife, cut into the wood along the line that indicates the position of the right arm.

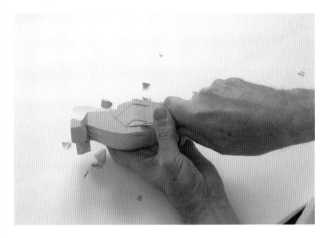

10 Still using the tip of the knife, cut into the wood opposite the previous cut and toward it at an angle.

11 A diamond-shaped wedge will pop out of the cut. Continue to widen the cut until you reach the edge of the blank.

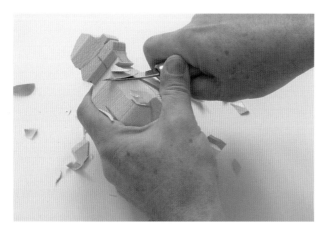

12 Remove large slivers of wood from the line for the pants pocket up to the head.

13 Clean up the cut at the bend of the arm so the arm is square to the body.

14 Notch the crease in the shirt sleeve at the bend of the arm; then knock the sharp edge off the body.

15 Remove the wood from the underside of the forearm by making a stop cut along the line. Cut in from the back to remove a large chunk of wood. Repeat this step as often as necessary to remove an appropriate amount of wood.

16 A series of slicing cuts is made to remove the wood from the back of the arm. A single cut across the bottom of these cuts will remove all of this wood. Notice also the clean cut under the forearm.

17 Make sure this cut is square before you move on to the next step.

18 Repeat the cuts that define the bend in the arm, the back of the arm and the underside of the forearm on the opposite side.

19 A view from the back at this point shows the cuts that shape the back of the arm. Notice how it seems that only several large, flat cuts were made to carve this area.

20 Remove small amounts of wood in long, curving cuts from the front of the piece to round off the sides. These cuts begin to shape the body.

21 The piece should look like the figure in this photograph at this point in the process.

22 Using the tip of the knife, cut straight in on the line that marks the pocket of the pants.

23 Remove a wide sliver of wood down to that cut.

24 Square up the bottom of the cut.

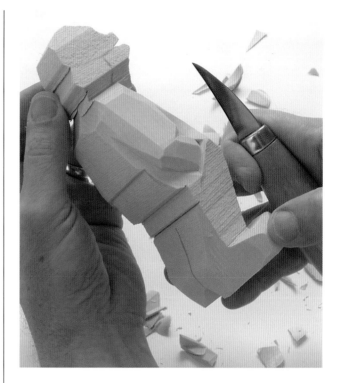

25 Cut a thin slice of wood from the sleeve to remove the bandsawed surface.

26 Two views from the side show the finished arm. Notice the crisp, clean angles and the long, flat cuts that give shape to the arm. Notice also that this shape is conveyed without any rounded surfaces.

27 Remove the bandsawed corner from the fronts and backs of both legs. These are long cuts that start just below the pants pocket and end at the ankle. Make more than one cut if necessary to reach the depth shown here.

28 Make a v-cut to remove wood at the seat of the pants. Here the left side is complete; I am working on the right side.

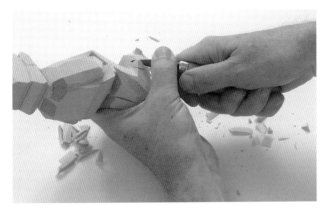

29 Slice a wide v-cut just behind the toes. This starts to give some shape to the shoes.

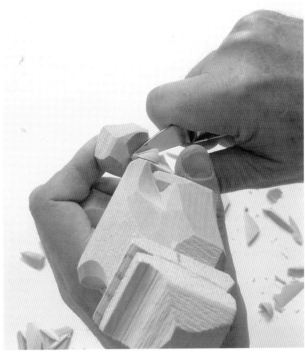

30 Remove wood to form the tops of the shoes.

31 Stop to check your progress against this photograph. Notice the long cut on the front of the leg and the flat planes that give shape to the shoe.

32 Make a large v-cut in the back of the leg to show the bend of the knee.

33 Redraw the line that separates the legs; then cut along this line with the tip of the carving knife.

34 Cut in at an angle to this line, removing a long sliver of wood.

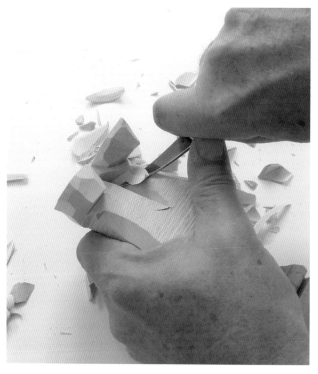

35 Remove wood from the front of the leg just above the ankle.

36 Make any additional cuts as necessary to create the roll of the pant leg over the top of the shoe. The shoes are now finished.

37 Continue working on the legs. Remove long slivers of wood to shape the legs. Remember, you want to make as few cuts as possible to create the overall shape.

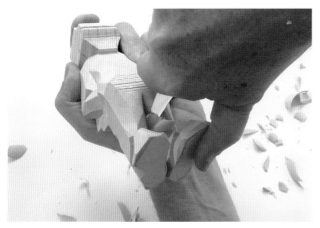

38 Remove additional wood from between the legs to separate the legs.

39 A small amount of wood is removed from the front of the pants, just enough to remove the bandsawed surface.

40 Make a v-cut in the crotch at the seat of the pants.

41 Clean up the seat of the pants so this area is square to the legs.

42 Remove wood from between the legs to separate them.

43 The toes of the shoes need to be raised slightly off the surface of the table upon which the figure stands. To do this, remove small amounts of wood from the bottom of the shoes.

44 Carve the notch that indicates the heel of the shoe.

45 Here you can see the difference between the raised shoe (on the left) and the unraised shoe. The shadow created under the raised shoe adds a bit of realism and interest to the piece.

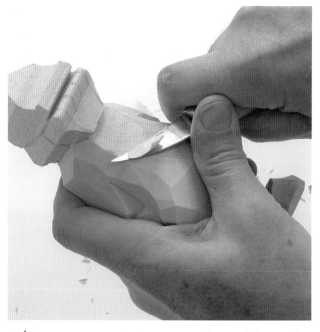

46 Remove a small amount of wood from the chest, just enough to clear away the bandsawed surface.

47 Make the v-cut that separates the hand from the sleeve.

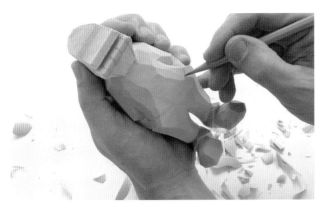

48 Draw the line that separates the pants from the shirt.

49 Cut in on this line with a knife; then remove wood above and below the stop cut to define the separation between the pants and the shirt.

50 Repeat this process to show a separation between the pants and the shirt on the back of the figure.

51 Remove wood below the cut so that the shirt stands out above the pants.

52 Make sure the cuts are perpendicular before moving on to the next step.

53 Remove wood from the back. Knock the corners off; then, remove a small amount from the center of the back, just enough to clean away the bandsawed surface.

54 Remove the wood from the shoulders.

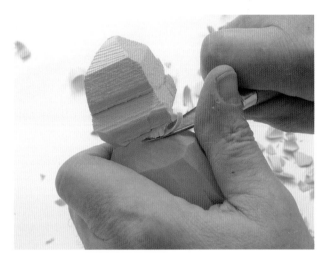

55 Clean up the cut where the shoulders meet the head.

56 At this point, take a few minutes to look at the carving from all sides. The back of the carving should look like this.

57 Begin work on the hat and the hair by making a v-cut at both back corners of the hat.

58 Continue the v-cuts around the sides of the hat. These cuts begin to define the separation between the hat and the hair.

59 Remove wood below the v-cut to shape the hair.

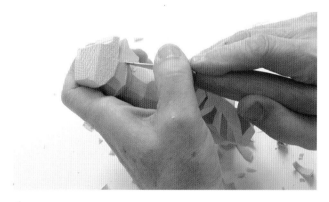

60 Using the tip of the knife blade, make a stop cut where the hair meets the face.

61 Remove wood from in front of the stop cut. This cut will make the width of the face narrower than that of the hair.

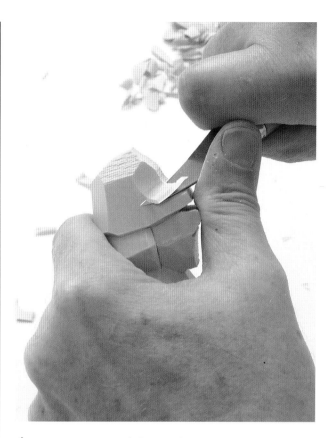

62 Remove wood from the hat. Remember to keep the number of cuts minimal. The shape of the hat should be formed by several flat-plane cuts, not by many small cuts.

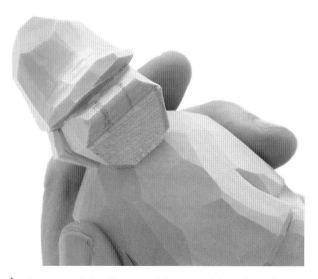

63 A shot of the face and hat to this point shows the effects of the flat-plane cuts.

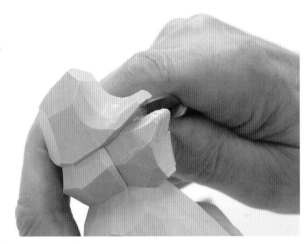

64 Remove wood from under the bill of the hat.

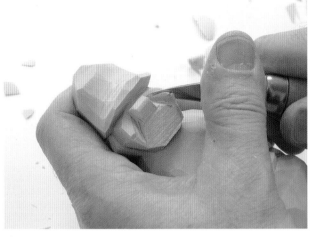

67 Use v-cuts to remove wood from these areas. The cut on the left is finished.

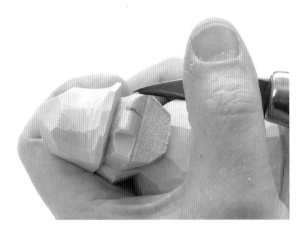

65 Cut in at the top and side of the face to remove the wood beside the nose. The finished cut is shown on the right side of the figure's face.

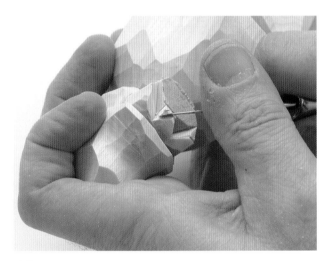

68 Bring the nose to a point by removing a triangular piece of wood from both sides.

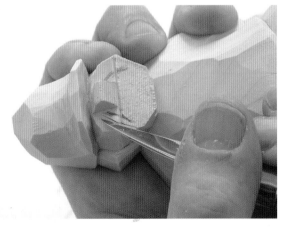

66 Draw lines for the cheeks; then cut into the wood at an angle along these lines.

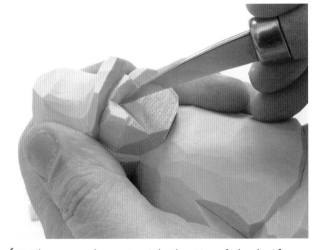

69 Clean up the cut with the tip of the knife.

70 Using a pencil, draw the smile.

71 Carefully cut the smile using small, controlled stop cuts.

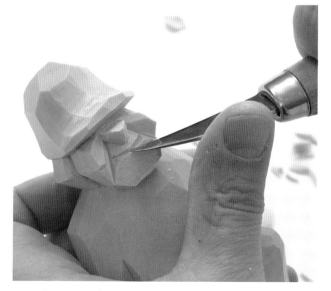

72 Clean up the cut with the tip of the knife.

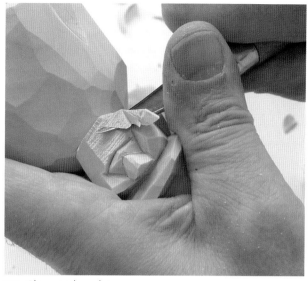

73 Shape the chin.

74 The main features of the face are now complete.

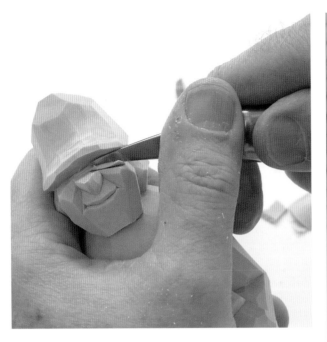

75 Make a v-cut to create the slit for the eye.

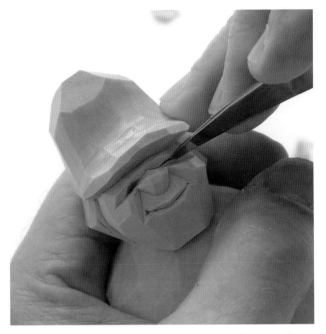

77 Using the tip of the knife, cut a deep hole in the center of the slit to indicate the eye.

76 The finished cut should look like this. Repeat this cut on the other side.

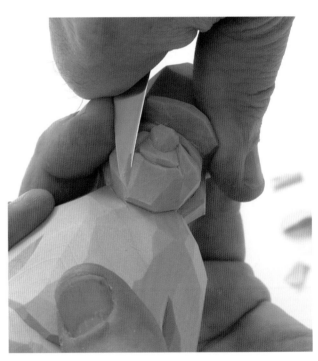

78 Make some final cuts to finish shaping the chin. These cuts should be made on both sides of the chin and below the chin.

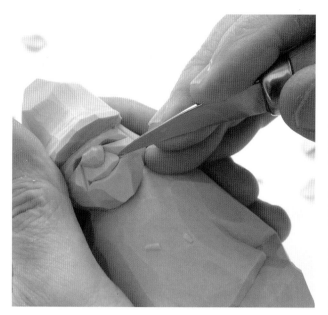

79 Deepen the ends of the smile.

80 Add the final details—wrinkles at the corners of the eyes, v-cuts for hair, lines to indicate a tie and a shirt collar—and the figure is ready to paint.

Painting a Traditional Flat-Plane Figure

Harley mixes the paints to about a 10:1 ratio of water to paint.

1 Mix black and brown iron oxide acrylic paints to create a dark brown color. Thin the paint to a wash with water. Using a flat brush with a chiseled edge, apply this color to the pants.

2 Add a little more black paint to the dark brown wash. Apply this color to the shoes and the hat.

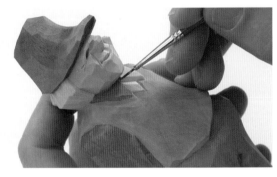

4 Paint the shirt with a wash of five parts Tomato Spice (Delta Ceramcoat) to one part brown iron oxide. Use a large brush to paint the sleeves; a smaller brush works well for the shirt collar.

3 Create a new wash of Norsk Blue (Delta Ceramcoat). Apply this color to the vest. Avoid slopping paint onto the shirt and hair.

5 Paint the hair with a wash of Crown Gold (Apple Barrel Colors Craft Paint).

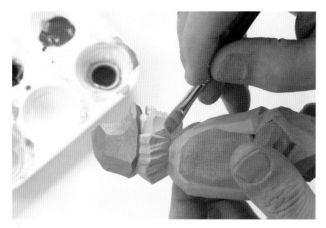

6 Paint the face with a flesh color straight from the tube. Choose either a pre-mixed flesh color from your favorite acrylic paint manufacturer or mix your own by combining yellow, red and antique white in a 2:1:4 ratio.

7 While the flesh color is still wet, apply a daub of Tomato Spice (Delta Ceramcoat) straight from the tube to the figure's nose and cheeks.

8 Blend the colors with a small flat brush. If the red color is too strong, wipe some of the paint away with a dry lint-free cloth.

9 When the paint is completely dry, brush on a coat of Johnson's Paste Wax. Use a toothbrush to scrub the wax into all of the nooks and crannies.

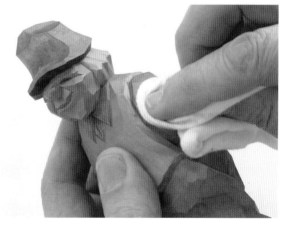

10 Immediately buff the figure with a lint-free cloth to a high shine.

11 Be sure to remove all of the wax. Wax that is not buffed away and dries on the carving will leave behind an unsightly finish.

The finished Oskar.

CHAPTER FOUR

Patterns

❖

Now, with two completed figures (from Chapter Three) looking on admiringly, providing inspiration and encouragement, it's time to expand and build on what you already know.

This chapter features patterns for additional figures, together with a bit of background on some of the characters, and suggestions for finishing techniques.

In order to fit all the patterns onto the page, some of them have been reduced in size from my original designs. Note that a grid has been drawn over the pattern. If you enlarge the pattern so that each square in the grid equals 1", you'll have the pattern restored to full size. You can reduce or enlarge these patterns as much as you like.

You should also feel free, as you gain more confidence, to customize or modify these patterns. For instance, if you want Oskar to hold a hoe or fishing pole in his right hand, refer to Johannes (p. 88) for an example of a right hand extended rather than thrust into the pocket. Or, conversely, if you prefer to exclude an element or two from one of the patterns, feel free to do that as well.

Oskar as a college graduate, in cap and gown? Willie (p. 113) with a hat? Why not?

Scandinavian Kick Sled, by Harley Refsal.
(From the collection of Walter and Marcia Sanders,
Jamestown, North Dakota.)

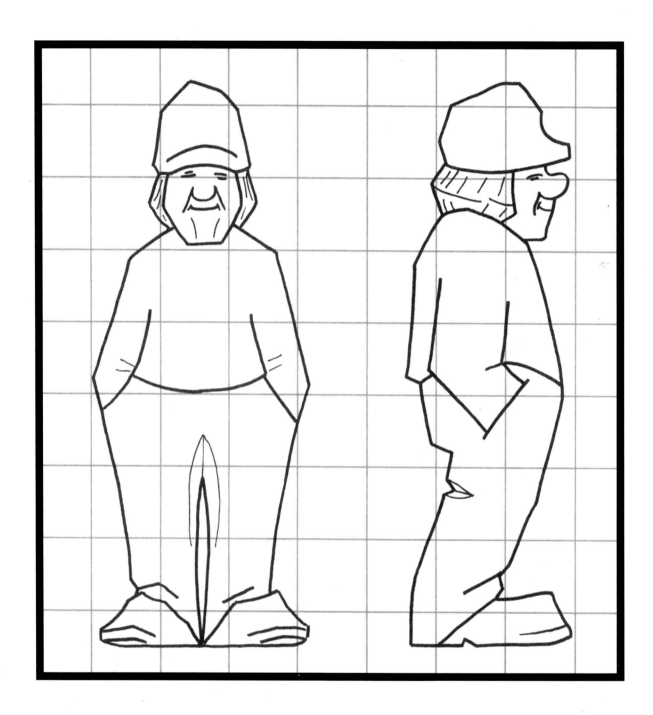

OSKAR

The step-by-step photos in the previous chapter show how Oskar is carved. For carvers who have never carved in this flat-plane style or for people who have never carved at all, this figure is an appropriate beginning project. His hands are in his pockets and his ears are covered by hair, relieving the carver of worrying about details while becoming familiar with this style.

As with most of these figures, the colors used for Oskar are muted earth tones. See the previous chapter for color suggestions.

Oskar and Sara (see opposite page) were the first in their Scandinavian community to immigrate to America, leading the pack about a century ago.

SARA

After a stormy crossing and a seemingly endless train ride, Oskar and Sara finally arrived at their new home, a recently settled community in western Minnesota. Here we see Sara wearing the clothes in which she arrived. Her scarf was probably brown or red iron oxide, her cape dark brown or black and her skirt brown or dark blue. Since her clothing was undoubtedly made from rather heavy handwoven material,

large, flat planes are appropriate for it. Her face can initially be carved in the same way as Oskar's, but then the rough, angular features should be rounded, either with a knife or a gouge, to give her a softer, more feminine look. A deeply rounded gouge, approximately ¼" wide, can also be used to make some random vertical grooves in her skirt to create the impression of flowing material.

JOHANNES

Although Oskar and Sara decided to emigrate, nearby cottagers Johannes and Kristina (see opposite page) were not able to take that step. Their economic plight was no better, but family commitments made the move impossible. However, after a while, their economic conditions did improve, partially because almost half of the population in their community eventually left for the United States or Canada and the pie no longer had to be divided into quite as many pieces.

Johannes is holding a homemade pitchfork, made entirely of wood. Starting with a naturally formed branch that serves as the handle and middle tine, matching tines are then whittled and pegged onto the handle, resulting in a three-tined pitchfork. His left side, with hand in pocket, is carved according to the same general instructions as for Oskar's pocketed hands. When carving his wooden shoes, refer back to the photo on page 13. Once again, dark, muted earth tones would be the most appropriate colors.

KRISTINA

Kristina is out raking hay. The handle of her wooden rake is inserted through the 3/16" hole drilled through her right hand. The rake's teeth are whittled pegs inserted into 1/4" holes in the head of the rake. Kristina's left arm simply hangs at her side. She could be wearing an off-white apron, a dark-green or brown skirt, a beige blouse and a red iron oxide scarf.

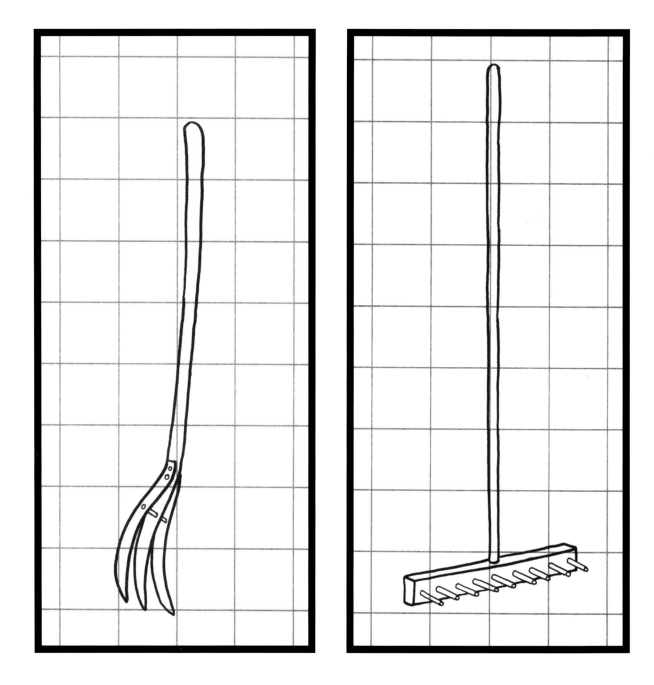

JOHANNES' PITCHFORK

KRISTINA'S RAKE

NISSE MOR

The Nisse Mor (*mor* means mother) featured here can have a gouge-grooved skirt, described in the instructions for carving Sara on page 87. Note that her face is not rugged and angular but softly rounded. Her hands are tucked under her apron, which can be decorated with stripes or floral designs. Her hat could also be decorated, perhaps with a border near the bottom. The colors could be somewhat brighter than those on an immigrant figure, but earth tones would still be most appropriate. (See page 49 for color suggestions.)

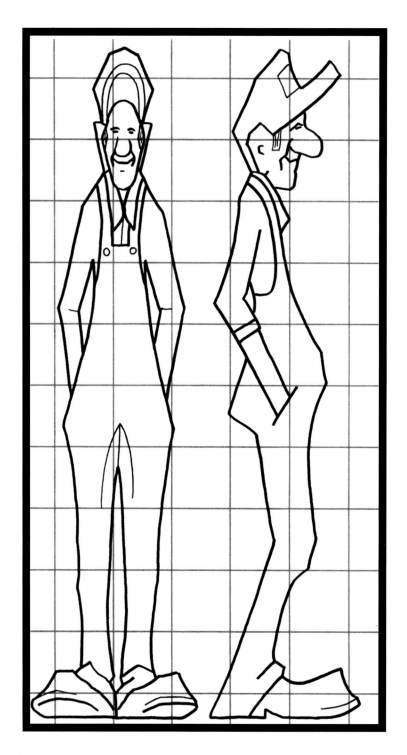

THIRD GENERATION IN AMERICA

He attends the Scandinavian festivals and celebrations in the Midwest without fail. Nordic Fest, Høstfest, Lutefisk Days, Midsummer—he wouldn't miss them for the world. Although he has never been to the Old Country, he's proud to be one of its sons.

He gets carved in a similar way to the other male figures on the preceding pages. His heels should be close together, with this toes pointing out. To aid in removing wood from between his arms and body, a small hole can be drilled to get started. Color choices could include a muted blue for his bib overalls, red for his shirt and green for his seed cap. This fellow requires a piece of wood measuring 3" x 3" x 11" but, of course, can be scaled down if you prefer.

ICE FISHERMAN

To be able to sit out on the ice like this for hours at a time, one needs to invoke the spirit of St. Halvor the Patient, patron saint of woodcarvers and fishermen.

This fisherman and bucket can be carved as one piece, or the bucket can be sawn off, carved separately and the figure seated on it after the carving is completed. The latter method makes it much easier to access the back and inside of his legs during the carving process.

Carve a separate piece for the fishing pole, and insert it into a 3/16" hole drilled into his hands as shown. Also, small holes can be drilled into opposite sides of the wide end of the bucket, into which ends of a piece of wire can be inserted, forming a handle.

After having been painted in earth tones (although he could be brightened up a bit with a red scarf) and oiled, he can be mounted on a base of your choice. Drill a tiny (no larger than 1/16") hole through the base, and string a length of elastic thread through the hole. Tie one end to the end of the fishing pole to indicate a fishing line. Draw the thread snugly through the base and knot it underneath. This will give the line a taut look, as if there were a lead sinker or bait on the end.

WOODCHOPPER

This woodchopper is determined. No hair is visible on him since his arms touch the sides of his head, and only his cap shows from the back because it runs all the way down his collar. His hands should be left large and stylized to provide ample material for the hole (marked with dotted lines) through which the axe handle will go. After drilling a tiny pilot hole through his hands, enlarge the hole to 1/4". Once the axe is carved, cut off about 1/2" of the axe handle (the flared end) and insert it into the hole from the top of the carving. The axe should be inserted so that the head is down and near his back. This position guarantees a powerful swing. One way you can create buttons on this figure is to drill holes (no larger than 3/16") and insert round, whittled pegs.

LOGGER

The timber stands of the upper Midwest, Pacific Northwest and Canada provided employment for countless Scandinavian immigrants, such as Karl. Here, he's holding a cant hook, which can be carved separately and inserted through a 5/16" hole drilled through his hands as shown. The wooden cant hook handle can be either left unpainted or painted a dark yellow ochre. The metal fittings on the cant hook can be steel blue or gray. Karl could be wearing a black cap, red shirt, brown trousers, off-white or gray socks and dark brown boots.

BRINGING IN THE FIREWOOD

Walter, here, has no time to stop for anything. He's got to bring in the wood—one of the most important chores of the day.

Carve the figure without his cargo. This allows access while carving his face (which is visible from the side even after the firewood is added) as well as his chest, the top of his arms and the inside of his mittens.

After painting the figure in colors of your choice, add the pieces of firewood, which are carved individually and glued together in his arms.

READING

Even though her days were filled with hard work, Eva savored those moments when she could sit down with a book. One of her brothers worked on a ship, and through her reading she got to travel with him, sailing to exotic ports of call, brimming with sunshine and fresh fruit.

The log bench is carved separately. Drill four 1/4" holes into the log seat, as indicated, and insert the whittled legs. Paint her clothing in muted earth tones of your choice.

NISSE

As with his Swedish cousin, the tomte, this Norwegian nisse is the bearer of Christmas gifts in his country. Dressed quite regally here, he looks almost like Father Christmas, with his red coat and hat trimmed with white. His beard and hair are also white, but different texturing on the hair will distinguish it from the trim. (Use a v-tool on the hair and a small rounded gouge to texture the trim.) His clogs can be painted yellow ochre, darkened slightly with brown.

THE SCHOOLTEACHER

Miss Barrows began teaching in a one-room country school when she was seventeen, and she continued teaching in various schools for the next hundred years. At least, that's what it seemed like to her pupils. She could be tough, but her severity was tempered by those occasions when she would hold the entire second grade (both of us) on her lap during reading. She usually wore a black or dark brown skirt and an off-white blouse.

DOWN A QUART

This is Sparky, a gas station attendant of an earlier era. He was there to fill the tank, check the oil and tires, clean your windshield and fill you in on everything from driving conditions and weather reports to sports scores.

His pants can be painted either blue or olive green. His shirt and cap, perhaps featuring the logo of your favorite service station, can be painted white or "company colors."

THE GARDENER

When May rolls around, Gus gets his hoe out of the tool shed and begins to commune with nature, carefully tending those plants and seedlings he's been thinking about since February.

Drill a 3/16" hole through his hand and insert the hoe, which is carved separately. The blade of the hoe can also be carved separately and then glued onto the handle.

Outfit him in subdued colors of your choice. You may want to paint the metal portion of the hoe a bright color, such as blue, green or red.

ALLELUIA

Rev. Carlson has a rather firm grip on his emotions. You'll probably never see him doubled over with laughter or shouting loudly and inappropriately. But what is more important is that he's there through thick and thin—celebrating, grieving, tending his flock.

His clerical shirt is black with a white collar. Using either glue or wood screws, mount the bust on a wooden base of your choice.

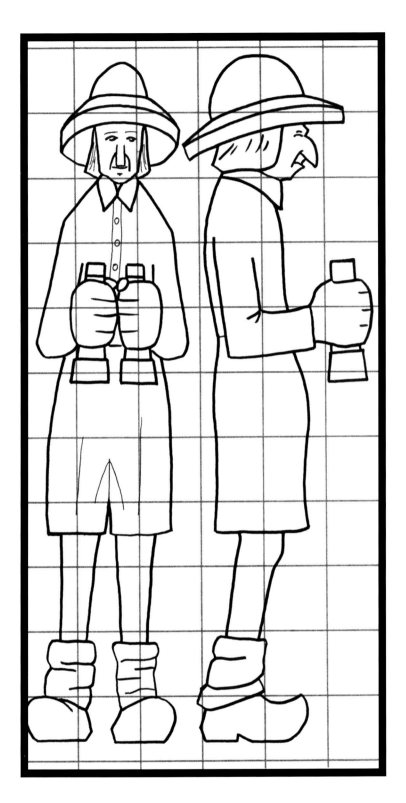

THE BIRD WATCHER

Just as some dog owners eventually begin to resemble their pets, the beak on this bird watcher is becoming more pronounced with each passing migration.

A khaki-colored uniform would be appropriate. The pith helmet and socks are off-white, the shoes are brown and the binoculars are black.

THE AUDITOR

"I'm here to take a look at your books." Dressed in a black or dark blue suit, this auditor presents a severe image.

His briefcase, sawn from 1/2"-thick stock, can be carved separately. Drill a 3/16" hole through his hand to accommodate the handle, which can be made from either two pieces of wood, carved and glued into place, or from a piece of leather shoelace. If you prefer the leather handle, drill two 1/8" holes into the top of the briefcase; then thread a leather shoelace, cut to the appropriate length, through his hand and glue both ends into the holes in the briefcase.

ED

Ed lives in a river town and has worked on riverboats nearly all his life. Note that his head is turned slightly to one side. He's watching a neophyte pilot trying to dock. The smirk on his face suggests that HE could do it better, and he enjoys watching the young whippersnapper sweat. Ed usually dresses all in black. If you prefer to see Ed wearing a different kind of cap, simply leave more wood on the top to accommodate different headgear.

HERBERTINE

Back in the Old Country, before they immigrated to North America, her parents wanted a son; they already had four daughters. They had even chosen a name for their son-to-be: Herbert. But then came daughter #5...so they named her Herbertine (her-burr-TEEN-uh). Her friends and family agree that her personality is as unique and wonderful as her name. Drill a hole through her right hand, as indicated, to accommodate her parasol.

OLAF

Olaf is another version of a nisse or tomte, the friendly little guy who serves as the bringer of gifts at holiday time in Scandinavia. Olaf typically wears a red cap with white trim, a yellow ochre (or blue or green) jacket, dark blue knickers, red socks and wood-colored clogs.

TOMTE WITH STICK

The Tomte (Swedish), or Nisse (Norwegian), is the bearer of Christmas gifts in Scandinavia. But he and his colleagues are around during other parts of the year as well. Back during the time when most people lived on farms, the tomte usually lived in the barn. If treated well, he could be counted on to help around the farm—but if mistreated or scoffed at, the tomte could also be mischievous.

This tomte has a walking stick in his right hand, not quite as tall as he is, whittled separately and inserted through the hole indicated in the pattern. The hole is 1/4" in diameter, but drill a pilot hole first. When drilling the hole, align it so that

the walking stick doesn't jab into the top of his foot but touches the ground just beside it. He also has a homemade backpack woven from birch bark. Using a V-tool or a knife tip, carve lines to indicate a basket-weave pattern.

His beard could be white, his cap red (with a red or white ball), his jacket green or red, and his mittens and backpack a golden color. (The white side of the birch-bark strips should face inward.) His shoes could be yellow ochre, brown or brownish-green, depending on where and how long he has worn them. (See page 49.)

TANTE TRINE

Tante Trine (TAHN-tuh TREEN-uh), or "Aunt Trine," comes to visit about once a year. She's a little old-fashioned, especially in the way she dresses (dark brown skirt, dark green coat, black hat with red trim), but the kids can hardly wait for her visits. They love her bedtime stories, as well as the box of fresh, homemade doughnuts she always brings along.

GOLFER

He may never make it to St. Andrews, but he tries to dress the part nonetheless. His sweater vest, shirt and argyle socks are all in pastel colors. You can make his golf shoes into saddle shoes, if you prefer. And finally, refer to a real golf club or putter as a model for the one you'll carve and insert through the 3/16" hole drilled through his right hand.

CHORE TIME

When Selma went out to help with evening chores (feeding the calves, milking cows—including sharing a little fresh, warm milk with the four or five barn cats—and closing the door of the chicken house for the night), this is how she dressed: blue jeans, dark green jacket and a red bandana-like kerchief.

CAPTAIN

Dressed in his dark blue uniform, brass (yellow ochre) buttons, white shirt and white or black cap (with black brim), the Captain always cut a striking image. Carve an appropriately-sized pipe if you'd like, which can be inserted into a 1/8" hole drilled at the very end of his mouth.

WILLIE

Willie was never much of an athlete, but he could run circles around other craftsmen in town when it came to the masterpieces that emerged from his woodworking shop. His ancestors, all of whom emigrated from Sweden, would have been proud if they could have seen his woodcarving, his scroll-saw creations and his lathe work. If you think Willie should have a bit more hair or a hat, leave some extra wood on his head and make him as hairy as you'd like.

RICHARD

Richard LOVES to chop wood. And he's good at it too. One whack and that 12"-long piece of oak flies apart. Ah…more firewood for the months to come. He typically wears a red wool shirt, a black cap (with optional yarn ball on top carved separately and inserted) and blue or green trousers…plus brown lumberjack boots. For a model of a hatchet or an axe, whichever you prefer, refer to p. 94.

LEPRECHAUN

Thanks to trips to Ireland by Vikings a thousand years ago, nearly every nisse in Norway or tomte in Sweden has a third or fourth cousin in Ireland: who else—a leprechaun. Painted in bright Irish green, with black shoes (ochre buckles), white socks and a carrot-colored beard, he has a walking stick inserted into the 3/16" hole drilled through his right hand.

BAKER

Gladys found steady employment as a "hired girl," helping busy farm wives with cleaning, washing and baking. Dressed in wooden clogs, red kerchief, dark green skirt, white blouse and off-white apron, her hands support a serving tray or breadboard (carved separately and glued on after the figure is painted). Carve an appropriately-sized pie, loaf of bread, cake, etc. to place on the tray. The baked goods she's holding could reflect your own favorite family recipes or ethnic/holiday food.

ONLINE

Erik likes to work at home, even though he doesn't have a very elaborate home office. Carve his body and the seat of the stool on which he's sitting together, all in one piece; then drill 1/4" holes into the underside of the stool and insert three or four pegs. Carve pieces for the taller chair and assemble the chair. Carve an appropriately-sized computer for Erik to use—what home office would be complete without one?

TROLL

Scandinavian trolls were once huge, menacing creatures—so huge, in fact, that the impressions left by their footprints, when filled with water, account for Scandinavia's many lakes. But through the years those trolls shrank in size, and now, 21st century trolls typically aren't more than about 20-24" tall. This one is even smaller, but his bare feet, unkempt hair and natural-branch (or twig) walking stick all still bespeak a critter of the wild. Although very soiled, his trousers appear to be dark green, and his well-worn flannel shirt was once red. Insert his walking stick into the 1/4" hole drilled through his right hand.

HANSEN

Despite his sometimes-unruly pupils, Mr. Hansen loved his job as a teacher. Book (carved connected to his body...not carved separately and inserted) tucked under his arm, clad in conservative black, he looks confident and ready to begin his day of teaching. Sixteen pupils, grades 1-8, await his arrival in the small one-room country school. It might sound quite rural and parochial, but Hansen opened their eyes and minds to a vast and exciting world: Marco Polo...sailing ships...migrating butterflies...pirates... mathematics...

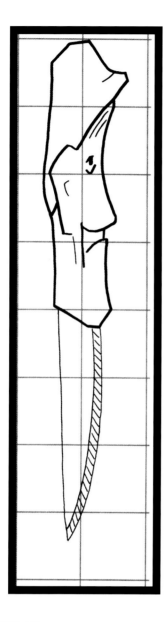

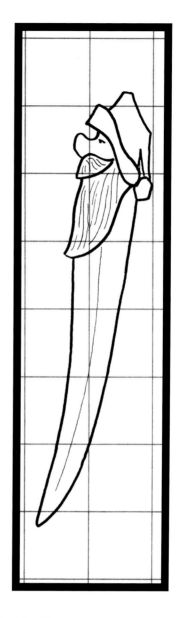

THE WHITTLER

There is plenty of room on the handle of this laminated Swedish Mora knife, sometimes also referred to as a Swedish carving knife or a sloyd knife, to carve something interesting. And if one intends to use the knife for carving or whittling, what better subject could there be than a whittler!

Transfer the shape of the handle onto a practice piece, perhaps a scrap of soft basswood or pine. Carve a prototype to make sure that despite its carved surface, the handle still fits comfortably in your hand. Also, if a different style of knife handle is being carved, facial features and proportions may have to be altered slightly from the pattern presented here.

Caution: Be sure to make a blade guard before beginning to carve a handle. (A double thickness of cardboard taped securely around the blade should do nicely.)

Once carved, the handle can be painted and/or oiled.

LETTER OPENER

Saw the letter opener from 1/4" or 3/16" material. Carve the head as shown, using a v-tool for detail in his beard, hat and hair. In shaping the blade, imagine a two-edged knife blade. The center remains thicker, but it thins down to form cutting edges on both sides. Paint the cap red and the trim and beard white. The blade can either be painted or left a natural wood color.

POLITICIAN

Senator Long has served for many terms. He runs on his name: Long on honesty…Long on optimism…Long on hard work, on behalf of the people of his state. He wears a navy blue suit, white shirt, red tie and black shoes. (If he takes off his jacket, you can see that he also sports red suspenders, a white belt and a very fat wallet.)

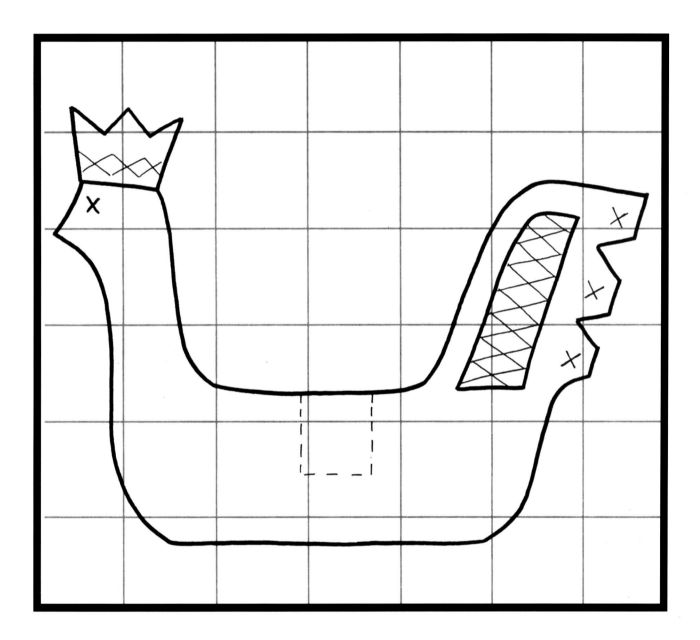

ALE HEN CANDLE HOLDER

The design for this candle holder is based on a traditional Scandinavian ale hen, described in Chapter One. Bandsaw the piece from 1 1/8"-thick or 1 1/4"-thick basswood or pine. Sand the entire piece, and then v-tool in the design as shown. Drill a 3/4" vertical hole (or appropriately larger, if you will be using brass candle holder inserts, available from woodcraft suppliers) for the candle. The piece can be left natural (finished with satin varnish or oil) or can be painted in colors of your choice.

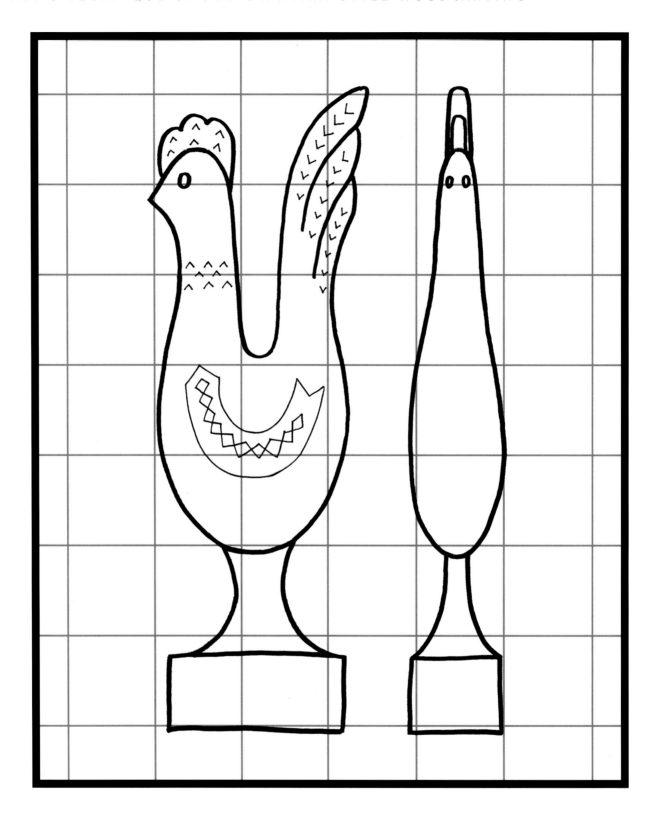

ROOSTER 1

Inspired by the traditional Swedish rooster featured on page 14, this modernized version can be decorated in a variety of ways. If left unpainted, it could be decorated with woodburning or chip carving. If painted, feel free to refer to design books, photos of painted eggs, etc.

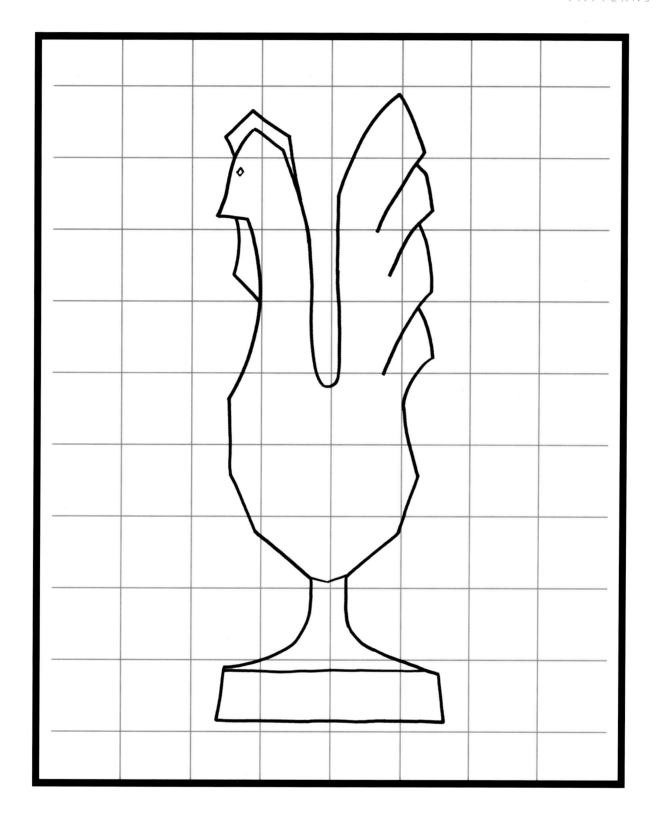

ROOSTER 2

Here's another version featuring slightly angular lines.

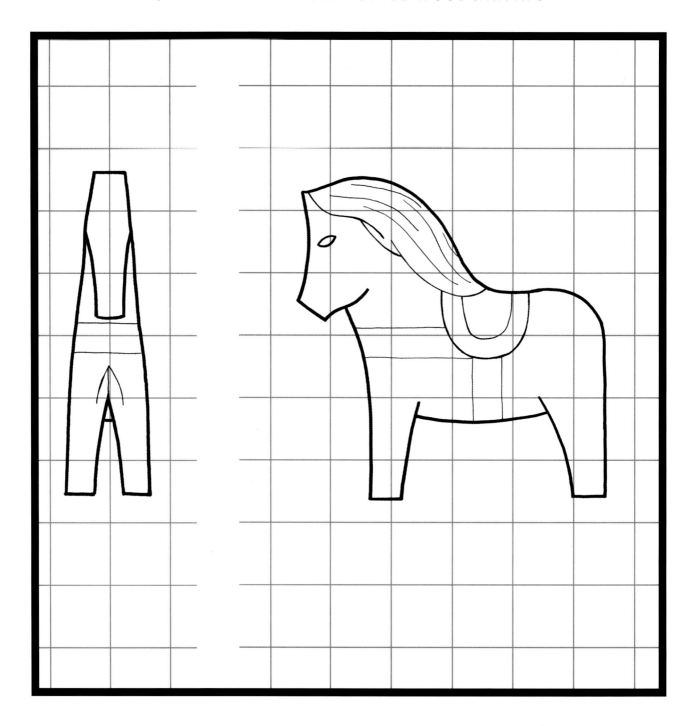

HORSE 1

Here's the pattern for sawing out the Dalecarlian horse featured on page 58.

HORSE 2

Pattern for horse featured on page 52.

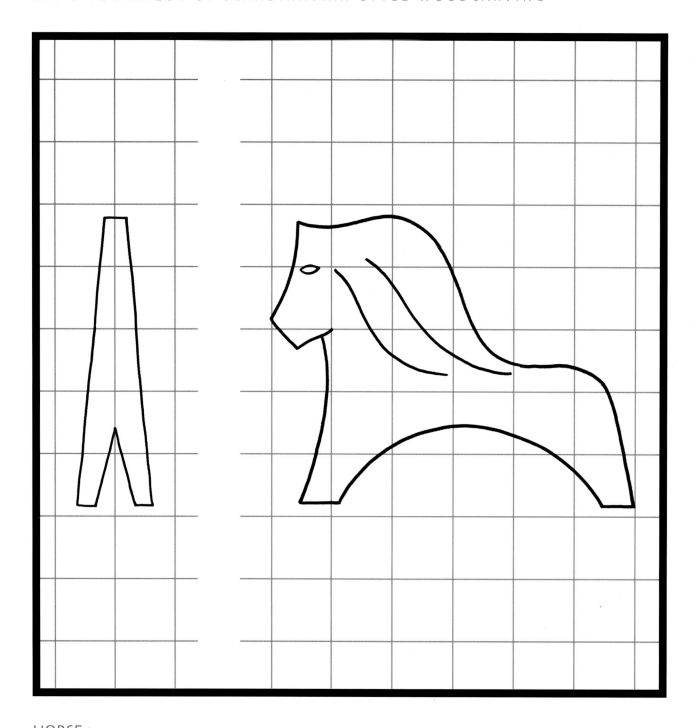

HORSE 3

HORSE 4

ORNAMENTS

The holiday ornaments here and on the following pages are sawn from 1/4" material. Drill a 1/16" hole through each ornament; the dot on the patterns indicates hole placement. Later, thread a cord through the hole to hang the ornaments on a tree.

Surface-carve the front side and sand the back. (Or, if you prefer, you can carve both sides.) Carve off the sharp corners so that the ornament resembles a cookie.

V-tool the design; then paint with appropriate holiday colors. Since I want my Christmas ornaments to help create a bright, festive atmosphere, I don't thin the acrylic paint with as much water as when I'm painting muted turn-of-the-century immigrant figures.

Finally, wooden stands can be made so that the ornaments can be placed on a shelf or table instead of hung on a tree. Rip a 3/4"-wide groove 1/4" deep the entire length of the strip. Saw the strip into pieces approximately 2" long. Sand the pieces on all surfaces, and they will make ideal stands for your ornaments.

MOUNTED NISSE

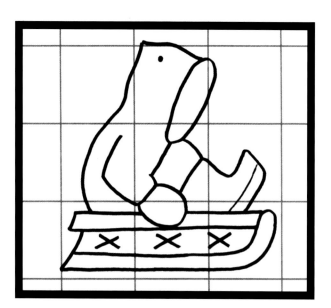

SLEDDER

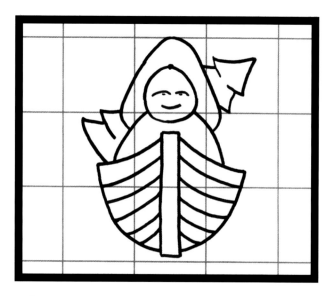

HOME FOR THE HOLIDAYS

HOLIDAY CANDLE HOLDER

Saw this piece to shape from 3/8"-thick stock. Drill a vertical hole to accommodate a birthday candle as indicated. (Based on the size of the candle you will be using, the hole should be approximately 3/16".) Surface-carve the entire figure, and then v-tool in his features as shown. His beard, as well as the base, can be painted white. His robe is red, and his cap and mittens can be either red or bright green.

TOMTE, OR NISSE

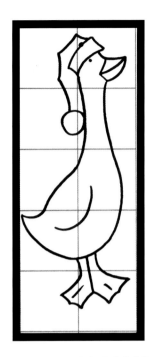

CHRISTMAS GOOSE

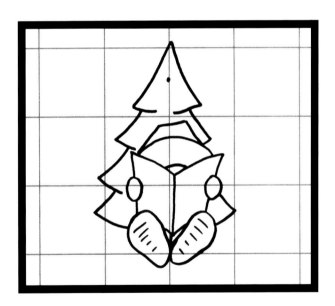

THE CHRISTMAS STORY

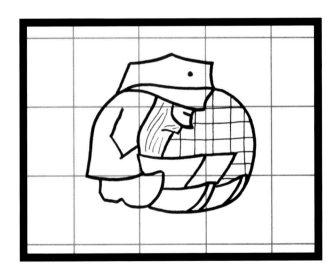

CHRISTMAS MORNING

Bibliography

Döderhultarn, Axel Petersson, and Det Är Något Särskilt med Trä, articles in *Hemslöjden 1991/2* (pp. 9–11) (written in Swedish). Stockholm: Olle Nessle and Mark Esping, 1992.

Figure Carving Scandinavian Style with Harley Refsal. 2004. Produced by Pinewood Forge, Leonard, MN. Videocassette/DVD.

Henning, Darrell, Marion Nelson, and Roger Welsch, *Norwegian-American Wood Carving of the Upper Midwest* (written in English). Decorah, Iowa: Vesterheim, 1978.

Magerøy, Ellen Marie, *Norsk Treskurd* (written in Norwegian, contains English summary). Oslo: Det Norske Samlaget, 1983.

Mosey, Chris and Michel Hjorth, *Magic Horse.* Stockholm: BOOX, 1999.

Nylén, Anna-Maja, *Swedish Handcraft* (English translation of *Hemslöjd*, written in Swedish). Lund: Håkan Ohlssons Förlag, 1976.

Rådström, Anne Marie, *Dalahästen* (written in Swedish). Hedemora: Gidlunds Bokförlag, 1991.

Refsal, Harley, *Carving Trolls and Other Scandinavian-Style Characters.* Decorah, Iowa: Dog Hill Press, 1995.

Weissman, Ira, and John Matthews, *Master American Woodcarver Emil Janel* (written in English). New York: New York Woodcarving Press, 1984.

Index

More Great Project Books from Fox Chapel Publishing

Complete Beginners Woodcarving Workbook, 2nd Edition
By Mary Duke Guldan
Any hobbyist new to the art of woodcarving will appreciate the easy-to-follow tone of this "made for beginners" book. Special chapter on carving miniature jointed dolls and teddy bears included!
ISBN: 1-56523-197-X, 64 pages, soft cover, $9.95

Carving Found Wood
By Vic Hood and Jack A. Williams
Inside this book you will meet some of our nation's most acclaimed artists that specialize in carving driftwood, burls, cypress knees and other forms of weathered wood. You'll learn their secrets to remarkable carving, be inspired by a stunning photo gallery of their work and be led, step-by-step, through a cottonwood bark carving of a human face.
ISBN: 1-56523-159-7, 96 pages, soft cover, $19.95

Illustrated Guide to Carving Tree Bark
By Rick Jensen and Jack A. Williams
You will never look at a tree the same again! In this book, you will learn the specialized technique of carving figures in tree bark. Included is a complete guide to the various species of cottonwood bark. A thorough step-by-step carving project of a magical tree house is included along with a beautiful gallery including woodspirits, animals, whimsical tree houses and much more.
ISBN: 1-56523-218-6, 80 pages, soft cover, $14.95

Caricature Carving from Head to Toe
By Dave Stetson
Find out what makes a carving "caricature" with this top-notch guide from Dave Stetson. First you will learn how anatomy relates to expression by creating a clay mold. Then, you will follow the author step-by-step through an entire carving project for an Old Man with Walking Stick. Additional patterns for alternate facial expressions, overview of wood selection, tools and an expansive photo gallery are also included.
ISBN: 1-56523-121-X, 96 pages, soft cover, $19.95

Whittling Twigs & Branches, 2nd edition
By Chris Lubkemann
With little more than a knife, a branch—and a dose of concentration—this book will show you how to create unique keepsakes that are fun to make, will be appreciated as gifts, or can be popular items for sale.
ISBN: 1-56523-236-4, 72 pages, soft cover, $9.95

Carving Golfers
By Bill Howrilla
Learn to carve golfers that look as if they could walk right off their wooden bases and continue their games on your desk top! These expressive projects offer joy and humor as they capture a golfer at the height of his emotional nexus. Includes step-by-step projects, 12 patterns and information on creating clay armatures and making patterns.
ISBN: 1-56523-201-1, 72 pages, soft cover, $14.95

Woodcarving the Country Bear and his Friends
By Mike Shipley
Not quite caricature, but not realistic, these humorous creatures are easy and enjoyable to carve. The book features 12 woodland creatures, including a bear and a moose, step-by-step instructions and easy-to-use patterns. A complete carving and painting project will teach you all the techniques you'll need to know to finish the other projects in the book.
ISBN: 1-56523-211-9, 64 pages, soft cover, $12.95

Extreme Pumpkin Carving
By Vic Hood and Jack A. Williams
A new twist on a classic holiday tradition. Learn to carve three-dimensional faces and scenes in pumpkins using tools as simple as kitchen knives or as complex as gouges and chisels. This is a perfect book for woodcarvers who are looking for new and inexpensive ways to celebrate Halloween, as well as a great book for Halloween aficionados who want to have the best pumpkin carvings on the block.
ISBN: 1-56523-213-5, 96 pages, soft cover, $14.95

CHECK WITH YOUR LOCAL BOOK OR WOODWORKING STORE
Or call 800-457-9112 • Visit www.FoxChapelPublishing.com